the book

of

simple

human truths

the book
of
simple
human truths

INSPIRATION, LOVE & WISDOM

Molly Friedenfeld
Illustrated by Cynthia Shepherd

SHE WRITES PRESS

Published 2013
Printed in the United States of America
ISBN: 978-1-938314-32-2
Library of Congress Control Number: 2013932194

For information, address:
She Writes Press
1563 Solano Ave #546
Berkeley, CA 94707

DEDICATION

This book is dedicated to...

My husband, Peter, for your loyal and enduring support, patience, and confidence in me during my journey to bring this book from the space of my heart to the space of these pages. You are my grounding rod, my redwood tree, my safe harbor, and my soul mate. I love you forever.

My sister and spiritual companion, Carolyn, whose enduring support through endless phone conversations, e-mails, and other sharing of conceptual and spiritual insights and synchronicities has helped me bring my thoughts and Divine Guidance to fruition. Thank you for choosing to share your own journey with me. Your heart is as wide as the ocean is deep.

My granddaughter, Hailey, for spreading your own version of fairy dust wherever you go. The Angels and I are forever grateful for all you do to bring joy to this world. You are my little magic magnet.

My children, Mallory, Maddy, Will, and Jake, for being the wonderful souls that you are.

My other siblings, Jeannette and Dan, for all the years of love and laughter.

The loving memory of my parents in Heaven, James Hershey and Helen Hershey. You taught me that life is all about relationships, not the material things that we cannot take with us when we leave this earth. Thank you for teaching me about simplicity, joy, and love. I know you are always with me.

INTENTIONAL PRAYER

*God, I pray that the messages of peace, joy, love,
and truth contained within this book will speak directly
to people's hearts to assist them in every way possible
from this day forward. I ask you to connect with your
healing love my heart and the hearts of all those who
hold this book in their hands. I pray that the wisdom
gained from reading it will motivate them to go forward
and spread love and wisdom to others.*

Amen.

SOUL COMPASS

*(upper left—truth, lower left—love, lower right—peace,
and upper right—joy)*

The Soul Compass is the compass our souls are following. Each quadrant represents one of the four foundational energetic pillars for life transformation—peace, joy, love and truth. When we infuse these energetic pillars into our beings, as we travel throughout our days, we go on to inspire others in many positive ways!

CONTENTS

Gratitude 1

Introduction. 5

PEACE
Growing My Spirit 11

The Spiritual Samaritan 33

JOY
Spreading Sunshine 65

LOVE
Living from Our Hearts. 91

Kindness Is Everlasting 117

Transition to the Light 143

TRUTH
Every Soul Deserves the Truth 175

Illuminating What's Behind the Curtain 197

Transforming Souls 217

Discovering a New Way to Love 233

All Roads Lead to God 257

Afterword. 263

Energetic Exchange. 265

About the Author 269

About the Artist 270

About the Photographer. 271

GRATITUDE

I wish to express love and gratitude to all the souls who taught me life lessons, inspired me, and illuminated and supported me through my journey of faith to put the message of peace, joy, love, and truth into words. I hold a place in my heart for all of you.

It is with deepest gratitude I thank **Cynthia (CJ) Shepherd**. You are a woman of many incredible talents, and I have utilized all of them during the creation of this book. I am indebted to you for your beautiful drawings that have captured the soul of each chapter.

I am also grateful for the endless faith and support you have provided during the creation of this book. I have the deepest admiration for your spiritual gifts, which have allowed me to connect personally with the Divine, my Spirit Guides, Angels, and family members and friends who have transitioned to the light, affording me the peace of knowing that my loved ones are with me always. You are a gentle soul and I am blessed to call you my friend.

Another who deserves gratitude from the depths of my heart is **Bobby Sullivan**. Bobby, you are a talented, intuitive energy worker who provided gems of priceless wisdom numerous times during the writing of the book. Your readings gave me incredible insight and kept me motivated to pursue my goal of bringing my soul's projects from the ethers to earth. My initial reading with you brought forth information that guided me in forming my own Internet radio show as one of the avenues for getting my message out to the world. Your succinct and truthful message about working on myself first and growing my spirit while enjoying my journey was the impetus that helped me find my joy, and for that I am joyfully grateful.

I would also like to extend sincere gratitude to my friend **David Keyes**. I am in awe of and inspired by your incredible photography skills that so beautifully captured the light and soul of each drawing in the book.

I would like to extend sincere gratitude to my editor, **Miranda Spencer**, for her gentle guidance and innate ability to know what I was thinking as she organized and simplified my concepts and helped me bring this book to life.

And last, I would like to extend sincere gratitude to my publisher, **Brooke Warner**, for providing She Writes Press as a publishing platform for women writers; one that allows an author like myself the opportunity to bring my vision to life and retain the purity of my message.

the book

of

simple

human truths

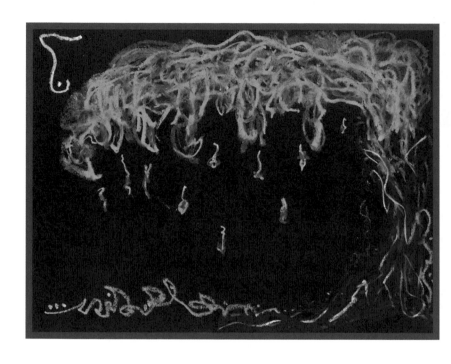

INTRODUCTION

This tree has taken a long time to grow into the magnificent structure it is now. It has received much on its journey
and now gives to others who are on a similar journey. Deep
wisdom from the Universe, not just the earth, has been its
friend and companion for ages, anchoring its roots and blessing its being. Now its roots run deep, allowing it to hold the
heavy overhanging branches full of the fruits of the wisdom
of the ages, some now dropping for others to gather, savor,
and use. Even the sap of the tree is oozing out of the trunk,
honey and balm for whatever souls scoop it up.

Introduction

I didn't have to travel to India to find God or myself. I stayed right here in the heartland of Minnesota.

My soul's journey in search of knowledge and wisdom began as it does for most folks, with major personal crises—job change, divorce, moving. But the revelation that changed the direction of my life, unexpectedly and irrevocably, came during the last few months, weeks, days and moments leading up to my father's death and after his transition to God's light. Helping him with love and compassion to transition peacefully opened my spiritual door and propelled me on a quest for further illumination and deeper truth, which in turn allowed me to remove my blinders and choose to see that there is much more to life than meets the literal eye. As I grew my spirit, I began to turn upside down all the things I had myself believed and been taught to believe by society and others since birth.

Thus I began a new journey, from my head down to my heart. It is from this benevolent location, the heart space, that I came to realize we are all divinely connected. We are all ONE. And we are here on earth to grow our souls and to encourage other souls to grow. I began to look beyond my ego, my family, and my circle of friends to realize a vested interest in all souls and found myself yearning to share learned insights.

Living from the heart invites in ancient wisdom I call *simple human truths*. I believe these simple human truths have been with us since the beginning of time, and are a gift to guide us and help us to attain Heaven on earth. This immense Divine Wisdom remains constant. It is humanity that has complicated it, twisting and distorting its purity by eliminating simplicity from almost every aspect of our lives and replacing it with complex formulas for superficial happiness.

Peace, I found, is simple. Joy is simple. Love is simple. Truth is simple. The things that make my heart sing, I learned, are the same things that my soul desires for me. And the things that are for my own highest good are also for the highest good of all. This means that by growing my spirit and becoming a better human, I am also helping humanity.

I came to that particular realization through recognizing and experiencing *synchronistic spiritual events*. As I will show you, there are no coincidences, only synchronicity, for nothing happens without reason in the Universe. Nothing. The Universe is guiding us with love behind the scenes, every single moment of our days. In this book, I'll recount how these epiphanies unfolded in my life, explain the simple human truths, share the wisdom I gained from lessons learned, and offer tips on how to apply this wisdom in your own life and in the lives of others.

My wish is that once this book touches your hands, the words you read and the pictures you see will land upon your heart.

Notes:

The word *God* is used throughout the book to recognize and humbly acknowledge the Creator. I invite you to insert the word(s) you feel comfortable using: Divine, Universe, Holy Spirit, Creator, Higher Power, or whatever feels right to you. I believe that regardless of our religion, we ultimately connect to the same Source of All That Is.

The words *Angel*, *Spirit Guide*, and other spiritual terms are capitalized throughout to show respect for the Divine.

In the stories contained in each chapter, individual names have been changed to respect that person's privacy; when a full name is used, permission was granted to do so.

Artist Cynthia Shepherd wrote the description of the soul art drawings located at the beginning of each chapter throughout this book.

Peace

GROWING MY SPIRIT

This soul has dropped to its knees in surrender and ser-
vice, having journeyed to the mountain where wisdom and
truth reside. It broadcasts its love and essence to the moun-
tain, which hears and amplifies the soul's field out into the
world. The soul's purpose is taking flight and this brings great
joy to the soul and all who receive it.

Growing My Spirit

Have you ever said, "I can't wait"? I can't wait until I get married…. I can't wait until I get divorced. I can't wait to go on this trip…. I can't wait to get back home. The essence of every journey is finding peace, joy, love, and truth in the process. Journeys never end, for once you get to your perceived destination, the next leg of your journey is revealed. Journeys are made of time fragments, time fragments turn into chapters, and each chapter of your life is just as important as the one you are living in this very moment. Embrace and enjoy each chapter of your journey as it unfolds, for this allows you to have the joy-filled life of your dreams, right here and now.

Road Construction

My path in search of truth and wisdom looks similar to that of any road you may come across in Minnesota after one of our agonizingly long winters. It has been riddled with potholes, detours, twists, and turns and is, I assure you, constantly under construction. But it is my path, and I'm the one with the choices before me, not only to repair the road I've traveled upon with the understanding of lessons learned, but also to set forth with new vision upon the road that lies ahead, the path I will travel on unmarred by time, travelers, or experiences thus far.

We human souls are a work in progress. Each today brings forth a new opportunity to learn something that you didn't know yesterday, and this process helps create in you a better person for your tomorrow.

My path is no more or less important than yours. My journey may look similar to or completely different from another soul's journey, but I guarantee that all paths, just like mine, are paved with lessons in peace, joy, love, truth, compassion, humility, judgment, faith, forgiveness, self-control, kindness, gentleness, and more. What each one of us decides to do with our lessons will determine how far we travel, how many lives we touch, and what our path looks like for this lifetime. There are no precise rules for how to live a human life; for each of us it is about choice. We all get to decide. For this reason, the only instruction manual we will ever receive contains one page, with one word: *CHOOSE.*

SIMPLE HUMAN TRUTH

We human souls are a work in progress. Each today brings forth a new opportunity to learn something that you didn't know yesterday, and this process helps create in you a better person for your tomorrow.

Soul Searching

A very important leg of my journey began back in 2000. I had a great job, a great family, great friends, and what I thought was a great life. I had been working as a continuity director at a

Minneapolis radio station, in peace with my co-workers and my current boss, for nine years. My plan was to continue doing things the "safe" way for as long as possible. The Universe, however, had a different plan for me.

The first hint I was headed in a different direction arrived in the form of a new boss who came in like a storm trooper on a plane from New York. The guy (I'll call him Stan) wanted everyone to know there was a new sheriff in town and that things would be changing now that he was in charge. Stan began dismantling our comfortable and caring office environment piece by piece, rattling the windows and shaking out the rugs with the wave of one corporate hand. Soon, our once family-like office environment began to feel sterile and impersonal. Employees in record numbers began finding ways to escape. I held on tight for another four years, one of the last original employees. I didn't like change. I didn't want change. But eventually it became too much of a burden to show up for work each day and, in 2004 with thirteen years of service under my belt, I retracted my hold, succumbed, and resigned.

After leaving the station, I decided it was time to get out of my comfort zone and try something totally different, with more freedom and fewer cubicles. I took a big risk and ventured onto an entirely new career path as a real estate agent.

By late 2006, my elderly father, who had been diagnosed with congestive heart failure, was not doing well. It was time for him to sell his home of forty-six years and move, but he didn't want to budge.

This process alone had its own set of new and unfamiliar dynamics. The process of moving an elderly parent from his home when he doesn't want to leave it is like trying to wrestle an alligator out of a Louisiana bayou: You might ultimately accomplish the feat, but it won't be without some battle scars or one less appendage. The control my father was trying to exert by holding onto his house when it was time to leave mirrored the control I had been exerting by holding onto a job that didn't serve me any longer.

Also around this time, my marriage to my then-husband was dismantling. We had been together for almost fifteen years, but it felt as if we were two ships that passed in the night. We loved each other, but were not *in* love with each other. We were not invested in our relationship. I wanted more and he deserved more. I was being gently pushed behind the scenes to leave the comfortable once again. I was also being guided to release my hold on worldly items; I realized it was time to sell the ten-acre hobby farm about forty miles from Minneapolis where he, my daughter Mallory, and I had lived since 2002.

I was learning that while it is not fun to leave the normal and comfortable, sometimes the Universe says, "Heads up, down there. It's time to change."

There I was, facing the kind of major life stressors psychologists and pharmaceutical commercials talk about. The difference? My major stressors were occurring all at once.

But with each difficult, unforeseen turn of events, something incredible happened. I didn't lose my mind, and I didn't fall into a deep depression. Somehow, somewhere from the depths of my soul, I could almost audibly hear words of encouragement. They went something like this: *"Stick in there. Ride this thing out. You can do it. Here comes another wave of emotion and pain, but have faith, for it too shall pass."* And do you know what? Eventually, it did pass. And then, something truly wonderful happened. My clenched fists, which had held so tightly onto the controls, trying to cling to the comfortable past and resist the inevitable—that word, *change*—finally began to loosen their death grip as I began to understand that what I had control over was absolutely nothing at all.

My life as I knew it was being stripped away like old siding from a barn weathered by wind and time. I creaked as the rusty old nails that once held me together popped from my wooden framing. I moaned and groaned as my foundation shifted with each new revelation of pure truth. I saw that the old me, the Molly I once knew and thought was pretty "put together," must be dismantled and left behind, for it was now time for greater things to emerge.

Yet, I can honestly say I never looked in the rearview mirror for fear of seeing my old self—palm turned up, index finger curling inward—beckoning me back as my mother did when I was a child gone astray. I didn't know much, but I knew that if I chose to stand still, paralyzed in fear of what lay before me, I could easily pivot on one heel and return to the past, my old ways, the old me.

Synchronistic events were beginning to play out daily, and sometimes hourly, helping me to shed the skin of the person I once was, or thought I was. The Universe was teaching me lessons, helping me to understand the importance of releasing my stubbornness and moving into my heart.

I have always had an intense love for animals, which is one of the reasons my family moved from the city to our hobby farm in the country. As my world continued to crumble around me and it came time to sell it, we still had three goats, fifteen chickens, two dogs, and three cats. Working through my inner battle with stubbornness and fear, I was completely distraught over the idea of having to find homes for all of these wonderful creatures that had brought such joy to my life. I had told my friends and family that no matter how long it took, I would not leave the hobby farm until all my beloved animals had found new homes.

15

Although I didn't yet know about the power of manifesting and the Law of Attraction (made popular by the book *The Secret* by Rhonda Byrne) I later realized that the Universe immediately began shifting energy, people, places, and events to make my statement true.

Within a few days, I arrived home from work to find a beautiful Husky wandering out on the busy country road by the end of our driveway. Being a dog lover, I brought it down to our house so I could call around in hope of locating the owner. Our neighbor across the street knew this dog's owner and graciously helped me by returning it to its home a few housing developments away.

Our farm was situated about 600 feet back from the road, so our chickens were allowed to roam freely, eating grasshoppers, bugs, and even wood ticks (yuck!). When dusk arrived, the chickens would meander into their coop in an orderly fashion and all I had to do was shut the door and say goodnight to my feathered friends. I appreciated the birds' beauty and bug-eating skills, and I knew they were grateful to me for their "free ranging" opportunities. It was a beautifully symbiotic relationship.

The following day I returned home from work expecting to put my chickens to bed as usual. Instead I found absolute carnage. My pet chickens had been massacred and strewn across our property. The Husky I'd saved the day before had returned, and when he'd seen the chickens his hunting instincts kicked in. I screamed in rage when I found my favorite, a rooster I called The Captain, lying by the door of our chicken coop. He was their patriarch, a true leader killed in the line of duty trying to protect his flock.

Then another tectonic shift occurred in me. This was the day I discovered my own personal mantra. I didn't need to go all the way to India to find it—I just needed to go a little cuckoo out in the country. My mantra burst from my lips in one big gasp of exasperation from deep down inside me: *"I'm just going to keep moving forward, one step at a time."*

I kept saying my new mantra over and over and over. If I encountered a setback, a painful event, or a person who asked, "How are you handling all of this and not losing your mind?" I would simply reply, *"I'm just going to keep moving forward, one step at a time."* It was *simple*, but heartfelt, and it saved my life. This *simple* mantra kept the light within me from going dark. This *simple* mantra gave me the power to chug ahead like the Little Engine that Could, even when my coal reserves seemed just about empty.

Within two weeks of my chicken tragedy two blessings followed. I found the perfect home for one of my cats and a friend down the street found someone who would take all three goats so they wouldn't be split apart. These blessings were followed by tragedy. I opened the door to the barn one morning to find my barn cat, Pepper, with an abnormal leg break. She had apparently gotten caught in a rafter and broke her leg high up by the hip socket. The veterinarian gave me two options: surgery, followed most likely by amputation of the leg, or euthanasia. I once again had more soul searching to do and chose what seemed most humane for both of us, euthanasia.

One by one, my animals were finding homes or being taken from me. The fulfillment of my earlier vow, "I won't leave the hobby farm until all my animals have found new homes," was being orchestrated and "taken care of" by loving Universal forces behind the scenes. It took a while to accomplish, but finally each and every animal had found a new home, here on earth or in Heaven.

Meanwhile, my life, and the person I once was, continued to change before my eyes. For months, a tragedy was followed by a blessing or a blessing by a tragedy. And in February 2007, my father took a turn for the worse and passed away. The next life-changing event was to actually place the hobby farm on the market. Everything I once held dear, including a sense of control, was slipping through my fingers.

I kept drawing power from my mantra, *"I'm just going to keep moving forward, one step at a time,"* and that's exactly what I did. My then-husband and I never did like drama and we agreed to separate, splitting everything evenly and leaving the lawyers and their fees out of our decision-making process. One three-hundred-seventy-five-dollar filing fee later, we settled our divorce, which was finalized in late 2007. At that time, I moved to a nice townhome closer to the city with Mallory and my granddaughter, Hailey (born in 2005), and finally felt some semblance of normalcy and order creeping back into my world.

Apparently, though, the falling away of my old life was not anywhere near complete. A few short months after moving to the townhome, my mother was diagnosed with cancer, multiple myeloma.

I will end my timeline of life-changing events here, because more stripping away of the life I once knew continued and continues to this day. My intention in telling this story is not for anyone to take pity on me, but rather to help you understand the soul-searching process as it unfolds. Each event in my life and yours is put in place to bring forth a new, compassionate, patient, forgiving, truthful, strong, and loving human being. This is God's wish for all of us who choose to discover the expansion that awaits us on the other side of our life events.

As I learned, this soul-searching process can be a peaceful transition if you allow it to progress naturally by finding your way to the truth early on and opening your eyes to Divine Wisdom as it's presented to you. Or it can be a long, painful, and arduous path similar to mine if you try stubbornly to control your destiny and remain in the comfort zone of blindness. My wish for you is a peaceful and beautiful journey of acceptance rather than an arduous journey of resistance. The choice to see will always be yours as each clue and lesson is placed on the path before you to decipher and absorb.

Powering Down the Generator

Though my controlled existence began unraveling in 2000, leading to a process of major change in my life, it wasn't until late 2006, during what would be my father's last few months on earth, that God finally got through to my almost impenetrable ego. Of course, He had been lovingly giving me Divine Guidance since my birth that I had, for the most part—with the exception of a few significant events—been ignoring or discounting as coincidences. The only difference was that now I was willing to see and listen—which also meant I was willing to learn.

Here's my deal. I had always been someone who liked forward movement and had prided myself on being the consummate multi-tasker. I was a doer and an over-achiever who didn't feel fulfilled unless my plate was overloaded with projects.

But during this difficult period, I really began allowing God to become an integral part of my everyday life. This openness allowed me to see the importance of shutting down my over-loaded circuitry and slowing down, so that He was able to get my complete attention for the very first time. I responded to the cue, and began to power down my internal generator, my brain, which always whirred at full speed, and allowed it to hum at a gentler vibration. During this slowing-down process, my father's health was declining further, reinforcing the importance of listening to my internal voice, which was guiding me to become even more aware of and more present for life's precious relationships.

Months passed; it was now February 2007. It became necessary at this time to move my father to a facility where he could receive end-of-life care. My family found a lovely hospice located on Twin Lake in Brooklyn Center, Minnesota, which he said felt like home to him. He spent his last weeks on earth there reminiscing, enjoying home-cooked meals, and looking at the wildlife outside the window of his room. He was comfortable, at peace, and knew he was loved.

After my father's arrival at the hospice, I began to understand that e-mails, phone calls, appointments, and laundry were inconsequential in comparison with being completely present for my father during this important time. This was the man who had always been there for me, and it was my turn to show him love with my undivided attention.

As I faced my father's approaching death, I was rewarded with time to sit and think about life. I was truly amazed at how I got to be so old before realizing that many of life's wonderful miracles reside in stillness and silence rather than motion and noise. I realized fast-forward movement had, at times, served me well in business, but it had also produced regret in the form of missed opportunities in many of my personal relationships.

SIMPLE HUMAN TRUTH

Many of life's wonderful miracles reside in stillness and silence rather than motion and noise.

During the final hours I spent at my father's bedside, memories of the times we had spent together came flooding back. I remembered being five years old, carried on his expansive shoulders down to Crystal Lake, by my childhood home, to see the Fourth of July fireworks. I could see myself as a bundled-up eight-year-old, standing in our backyard on a frigid March day watching him put the finishing touches on an enormous snow fort and slide he had built for us four kids. I flashed forwarded to another memory of myself as an eleven-year-old tomboy sitting on his lap in the car, our hands together on the wheel as he let me steer it down the street to deliver enormous Sunday newspapers along my paper route.

Reflecting back on the exceptional times I had spent with this great man created impressions that cemented in my mind that spending moments with another in earnest presence is one of the simple ways we can show unconditional love. It is the memories created from these impressions that survive after all else passes.

SIMPLE HUMAN TRUTH

Spending moments with another in earnest presence is one of the simple ways we can show unconditional love. It is the memories created from these impressions that survive after all else passes.

The Shifting Begins

After my father's passing, something shifted in me. Instead of going back to plowing through life with constant movement, I began to embrace more peaceful, patient, compassionate, and intentional living. I consciously made the decision to open the door to what lay before me with the intention of becoming more spiritually connected. I was amazed at how easily things began to fall into place during those rare moments when I stopped trying to control an outcome and instead allowed for new experiences and things to flow freely to me.

Each new day on my new path brought forth more memories: experiences, long-forgotten coincidences, past decisions, and discounted spiritual events to revisit and process. These memories came bubbling up to the surface one by one like primordial air bubbles in the La Brea Tar Pits. Once each bubble reached the surface of my awareness, it expanded, popped open, and plopped into my mind as another unit of important information to acknowledge and record to reinforce my learning. Each insight was brought forth in perfect sequence to show me that everything since my birth had been divinely orchestrated to assist me in my spiritual awakening, steering me to my path to help me find and fulfill my soul's purpose for this lifetime. I now recognize as I look back over the years that there were many jumping-off points, points of contact, and missed opportunities that were presented and dismissed, or that had slipped through my fingers altogether.

Point of Contact

Siblings (from left) Molly, Dan, Carolyn, and Jeannette

In May 2010 I received one of those points of contact, and this time I did not ignore it or discount it. I had been experiencing a string of real-estate bad luck: Even after all of my hard work and long hours helping clients, transaction after transaction fell apart. For a real estate agent, when transactions fall apart it means no pay—period, end of story. On this particular day, I had just finished showing twenty-two homes to three different sets of clients and was driving home when the call came in. It was another client, Andrea. I had being working with Andrea and her boyfriend for three months, hoping to find the couple that perfect home. Now she was calling to tell me her boyfriend's financing had fallen through and they would need to back out of their purchase, which was set to close in three weeks.

I ended the call and then the words came screaming from my throat without reason or thought: "What am I supposed to do?" I repeated, for emphasis: "Tell me! What am I supposed to do?"

Almost instantaneously, I heard my father's voice, ringing in my head loud and clear. It was as if he were sitting right next to me in the car. He said, "Don't you get in the car with another person."

I shook my head from side to side in an attempt to clear my mind, the way Scooby Doo, the cartoon dog, used to do when he came across a ghost during his escapades with Shaggy and their friends. This feeble attempt at mind clearing didn't accomplish anything, and ten minutes later I was still crying as I turned the corner into my neighborhood cul de sac. As I pulled into my driveway, I received a gift. My tears of frustration were replaced with a feeling that all would be well in the end. There, standing in my front yard, was a beautiful deer.

My father was very connected with deer during his time on earth. In fact, the day before my father's passing, as my siblings and I sat around his bed, we all watched as four deer crossed the frozen lake and came right up to his first-floor window at the hospice. They remained in front of the window into the night, gentle sentries of peace. When a beautiful buck showed up around 8 p.m. and joined the deer stationed outside the window, my brother Dan said, "Dad, a buck just showed up to guide you home." My family members and I knew that this was a spiritually significant event. It was truly magical.

Since he passed, the appearance of a deer is one of the ways my father communicates with me. Deer are a physical validation that my father's energy is with me. So I knew not to discount the deer in my front yard as a coincidence. I immediately acknowledged this second spiritual sign from my father, which had arrived within minutes of the first. My father was giving me symbolic, spiritual messages to help me move my life in a new direction, and I took them very seriously.

After this experience, I never drove another real estate client around looking for homes. I didn't let my real estate business fall apart, however. Instead, I went on to create a business plan and morphed it into a referral-based business in which I listed houses, found buyers, and then referred those buyers to my trusted real-estate friends for a fee. This new method of doing business without driving clients around freed up five to eight hours every day, which afforded me the time to focus on and figure out what I was being led to do with my life. It was one of my first conscious steps in seeing, listening, and allowing Divine Wisdom to flow new direction and opportunities into my life.

Preaching, Not Teaching

During this time, I learned and changed with each passing day. With a few more hours afforded me as a result of my new real-estate referral business, I progressed quickly. I began to notice more spiritual signs and synchronicities and became fueled with excitement. My exuberance and passion were overflowing and, for many, overwhelming. I wanted everyone to see the new person I was becoming and to hear about my spiritual experiences. I have never been a person who is at a loss for words so, believe me, I had a lot to say.

Unfortunately, I also learned quickly that not everyone was as excited about my message as I was. In certain situations I was preaching to the choir; in others, my message was falling completely flat, met with blank stares or immediate resistance. At the time, I thought I was helping people, but my words were actually having the opposite effect. My non-stop spiritual chatter was violating other people's personal boundaries. I was trying to cram *my* insights and newfound spiritual knowledge down the throats of those not ready, willing, or able to hear *my* message. I was preaching, not teaching.

My first piece of wisdom about the correct format in which to dispense information to assist others popped into my head in the form of a conversation from years ago. I received this "tidbit" of sage advice from a former landlord, who told me he'd heard it from a grade school teacher: "When you want your message to be heard, always speak from your heart and keep it short, because you have just thirty seconds to get your point across before their mind goes somewhere else." Basic and simple. "Pretty darn cool," I thought when I heard it the first time. "Brilliant, incredibly relevant, and tailor made for me," I reflected when I thought of it the second time, revealed in the form of a memory.

SIMPLE HUMAN TRUTH
When you want your message to be heard, always speak from your heart.

Fire Hosing

Over the course of the next couple of months, I began downloading more memories to reinforce this "keep it simple" concept. I remembered past instances when message-delivery methods I had been using on others were inappropriate and ineffective. Specific, random incidents began popping into my head in which I had "fire hosed" an unwillingly participant. (This is a phrase my friend Stephanie uses when a person opens their mouth to give someone "a piece of their mind," turning on a metaphorical fire hose full force to shoot out knowledge or opinions in a torrent whether or not the person asked for it or is prepared to hear it.)

Lessons about delivering information in a simple, teaching-not-preaching format and the importance of maintaining personal boundaries continued to roll in. Then, in July 2011, I was having a conversation with my sister Jeannette about the backlash I was receiving while attempting to talk about all the new knowledge and spiritual experiences I was gaining and knew in my heart I was meant to share with others.

As Jeannette began speaking I could see her words tumbling in slow motion, one word at a time, in my mind. The words then scrolled across my vision the way they used to move across the screen as I watched *Sesame Street* as a six-year-old child. I knew this profound message was being slowed down for me to present it in the way I learn best—by getting back to basics, right down to kindergarten level. As my sister spoke I breathed in and out a couple of times to lock myself into the present in order to hear, understand, and absorb each word.

Jeannette said, "No one likes being told what to do. If someone wants to hear a specific message, they will take a class, listen to a radio show, watch a TV show, visit a website or blog, or read a book."

This time, I received the message as it was being delivered. That wisdom-filled conversation with my sister was an essential piece of information I needed to process in order to connect the dots and see the big picture. It also foreshadowed many of the projects I would initiate within months.

I realized then that each one of us is given the choice to find and accept the truth within our own spiritual time frame. That is, once the truth is presented, it is our decision whether or not to recognize and retain the knowledge that has been dispensed right then and there, or to let it pass like a whisper in the breeze to return to it later in the form of reflection.

But when people are finally ready for knowledge and willing to receive the wisdom contained there, they will seek it out. This allows for peaceful learning. The saying, "When the student is ready, the teacher will appear" holds true. Just because I appeared didn't mean the person I was addressing was ready for me, and cramming a message down that person's throat just because it's what I believed they needed to hear was a boundary violation. I began to understand the incredible importance of respecting the paths of others by showing love and compassion for all souls' journeys. How I would get through to them was not by "fire hosing" with too much information and forcing people to see things my way. Instead, I began to see that I could most effectively help people by providing different avenues for them to find me, comfortably, on their own terms and when they were ready to hear my message.

SIMPLE HUMAN TRUTH

Each one of us is given the choice to find and accept the truth within our own spiritual time frame. Once the truth is presented, it is our decision whether or not to recognize and retain the knowledge that has been dispensed.

Violet

Soon after that poignant conversation with my sister, I got to work. A single thought popped in the very next day: "Why not create a name that gives meaning to the message I want to get out to others?" So that's what I did first. And in the silent stillness of one afternoon, I created the name that would encapsulate my life's mission and future work. My process was quite simple. I began by writing down all the words that flowed through my heart. I have always loved the color purple, but moreover I felt very drawn to the word *violet*. To me, the color violet, like purple, means honor, virtue, truth, wisdom, and spirituality, and is synonymous with faith and God. Amethyst is my favorite crystal. The tones and hues of purple contained within each crystal formation have always helped me feel an immediate spiritual connection.

Also, violet in the aura has special meaning. "Violets" are the inspirational visionaries and teachers who are here to help the masses. I have always had an inner sense that I was supposed to accomplish big things during my time here, to make a difference in this world. Upon learning the meaning behind the life color violet in the aura, I understood the reason I felt drawn to that particular beautiful color over all the others in the spectrum.

Wisdom

To me, the word *wisdom* means ancient knowledge. It's the kind of knowledge you not only see but feel when you look into the eyes of an elephant or stop for a moment to marvel at the deep wrinkles on its skin, both of which I believe contain the truths learned from each intentional step their feet and those of their ancestors have placed upon the earth. Wisdom is knowledge that is rich, deep, and everlasting. It's center-of-the-earth deep. It's center-of-the-earth pure. Compared with this wisdom, the knowledge humanity has come to trust and believe in is shallow and surface oriented. One can scratch away human knowledge easily with the toe of a boot to reveal the impurities that lie just beneath the surface. Pure *wisdom* is gained through the seeking of deep, pure truth. This wisdom is constant; it is never distorted, reshaped, or pieced back together to fit molds specific to a culture or its people.

SIMPLE HUMAN TRUTH

The knowledge humanity has come to trust and believe in is shallow and surface oriented. One can scratch away human knowledge easily with the toe of a boot to reveal the impurities that lie just beneath the surface.

Putting It Together

I took the two words, *violet* and *wisdom*, and put them together. "Violet Wisdom," I thought. "Now, that feels very right." The next step in this process was to Google *Violet Wisdom* to see if that domain name was available. The only thing my search brought up at the time was an event that occurred the same day my father passed away. That was my spiritual sign and the confirmation I needed to know I was on the right track. When your footsteps and thoughts carry you down the same path your heart and soul are directing you, you will know without a doubt that you are headed in the right direction. Within months I created an Internet radio show called "Violet Wisdom Inspiration Radio" and the Violet Wisdom blog, followed by the Violet Wisdom website. I was consciously and consistently following my inner guidance system, my heart.

I embraced the new concept of creating options and avenues, like the show and the website, that allowed people to be able to find the wisdom I wanted to share on their own terms instead of on mine. I was truly enjoying the creativity that flowed in behind this process. This new method of thinking and doing was reinforcement enough of the lesson that "fire hosing" another can be harsh and ineffective. "Brilliant!" I thought again. It is truly brilliant how the Universe lines everything up—individual items, events, and people—creating synchronicities that, like scenes in a movie, are part of the big picture that is our continued learning. Even the world's most talented movie director doesn't have the skill to do that.

SIMPLE HUMAN TRUTH

When your footsteps and thoughts carry you down the
same path your heart and soul are directing you,
you will know without a doubt that you are
headed in the right direction.

---

* * *

These were the humble beginnings of my journey in search of my inner peace and my true self—without having to travel all the way to India. The next chapter explains how, when you believe in the magnificent wonders the Universe places at your disposal and allow the energy of the heavenly Angels to assist you in your daily life, your heart expands—motivating you to begin making positive changes in your life and in the lives of others.

THE SPIRITUAL SAMARITAN

The green represents spiritual growth as well as new ways of being with each other that break through the cold dormancy of separation we have inflicted upon ourselves. Near the base of the green growth, wisps of snow still linger from the cold winter of the heart, but they will soon be gone. The seeds that were planted by our thoughts and intentions, watered by our tears and the sweat of our determination, have taken root and sent flourishing green shoots skyward.

The Spiritual Samaritan

*A Spiritual Samaritan lives knowing that if we were
to leave this world tomorrow, we were the best humans
we could be and we touched the lives of as many souls
as possible. We are not asked to be perfect. We are
asked to make a difference.*

Spiritual Samaritans in Czechoslovakia

*"Grandpa" Gerard Friedenfeld at 14 years old (center) with his
parents Henrietta (left) and Rudolph Friedenfeld (right) in 1939.
This was the last photo taken of Gerard with his parents.*

Years after my divorce, I married a wonderful man named Peter Friedenfeld. My new husband's father, Gerard Friedenfeld, was just fourteen years old on April 12, 1939 when the Nazis invaded the refugee camp in Czechoslovakia where he, his family, and six hundred other Jews moved after being ordered from their homes in Lundenburg, a small town in southern Moravia. The SS troopers singled out twenty-four men and boys for a practice called "exercising." The men and boys were kicked repeatedly and beaten with fists and iron bars. One of the troopers noticed a ladder lying up against a building and ordered Gerard to climb up the ladder and then jump off. He was forced to climb and jump, climb and jump numerous times until he broke his right leg. Fortunately, this ended the torture and he managed to crawl on the ground to the camp infirmary.

Shortly thereafter, two Spiritual Samaritans, a man named Mr. Drucker and a woman, appeared at Gerard's bedside. These adults gained permission from Gerard's parents to ask Gerard if he would like to immigrate to England. Gerard said yes that day. Another Spiritual Samaritan, Nicholas Winton, procured his release. Five weeks later, on May 31, 1939, Gerard Friedenfeld, along with one hundred thirty-five other Jewish children from two to fifteen years old, boarded a train in Prague en route to a port on the English Channel in Holland.

These Spiritual Samaritans were members of the *Kindertransport*, meaning children's transport, an organization founded in London in 1938. Kindertransport and its founder, Lola Hahn-Warburg, were responsible for saving ten thousand Jewish children from the Nazis and transporting them out of Germany, Austria and Czechoslovakia.

After that day, Gerard Friedenfeld never saw his parents again. He believes they were sent to Poland and most likely died during the artillery bombardment of the Warsaw Ghetto in April 1943. "Grandpa" Gerry Friedenfeld is now eighty-eight years old and has dedicated much of his free time to educating thousands of children and adults about the Holocaust.

Spiritual Samaritans are individuals who grow earthly Angel wings by extending love, kindness, and compassion to others unconditionally. When we extend ourselves to someone we may not know and may never see again, even if no one ever finds out what we did to help, that one encounter changes our lives and the life of the other spiritually, and forever.

SIMPLE HUMAN TRUTH
Spiritual Samaritans grow earthly Angel wings by extending love, kindness, and compassion to others unconditionally.

From Self-Centered to Soul-Centered Behavior

On the road to becoming a Spiritual Samaritan, there will be infinite opportunities placed in front of us to help us grow our souls. Soul-centered behavior creates a continuous forum for learning. It means we take the focus off of ourselves and extend assistance to another soul unconditionally whenever the chance arises. We are consciously invested in all souls. We move away from self-centered behavior toward soul-centered behavior. Living this way helps us to realize that whenever a soul crosses our path, it creates a relationship. It may be a relationship that spans a lifetime or last three minutes as you stand in line with someone at the grocery store. Understanding that each and every person has value and that each relationship is precious motivates one to become a soul-centered Spiritual Samaritan.

SIMPLE HUMAN TRUTH
*Soul-centered behavior creates a continuous
forum for learning.*

Conscious Humility

Conscious humility is the decision to live from our hearts. This state creates an opening for the wonderful and the miraculous to show up daily in our lives. We are humble, compassionate, and loving souls that create a space of love for all without casting judgment on another or expecting re-payment or recognition for kind deeds.

We become the creators of viral videos of inspiration that travel around the world. We create art, music and stories that demand re-telling and touch people in ways we never thought possible. We have within each one of us the capacity to become beacons of light for others. We are the earthly Angels known as Spiritual Samaritans: Lightworkers, difference makers, and demonstrators of compassionate love.

SIMPLE HUMAN TRUTH
*Conscious humility is the decision to
live from our hearts.*

Waiting in the Wings

On my personal journey I developed a way to initiate soul-centered behavior and conscious humility quite simply and effectively. I began talking to God daily. Through this communication and attending spiritual workshops, I learned that God gives us personal heavenly Angels and Spirit Guides to assist us in growing our souls. All we have to do to feel their Angelic presence is believe in and call on them. These wonderful beings of the highest light and love are always waiting in the wings to assist us on our journey through this life. ALWAYS.

I discovered that the more I believed in them, the more they made their presence known to me. The more I involved them in my daily life, the more peace and love I felt flow into me. And the more love I experienced, the more my desire to share this love with others grew, and the more *soul-centered* I became.

However, I also came to understand, this world is a dimension of free will. Angels and Guides are constantly guiding us by lovingly giving us clues to help us stay on our spiritual path, placing people in front of us to help us learn specific lessons, and making Divine Synchronicities occur on a daily basis. But in order for them actually to assist us with a request, *we must ask* them for their assistance and grant them permission to help us.

So, soon, my conversation each morning with God and all things Divine began with a simple request. I asked, "God and your heavenly Angels and Guides, please place someone in front of me today that I can help in some big or small way unconditionally. Thank you." Miraculously, almost every single day I saw the sign in a person or creature I was supposed to help.

Here are some possible ways you may be asked to help another soul or creature unconditionally:

- You may be placed in front of someone to give a piece of timely advice.
- You may be asked to do a big or small favor.
- You may save a life unexpectedly, or even unknowingly.
- You may see a chance to lend an ear, a shoulder to cry on, or a helping hand.
- You may be asked to donate blood or become a bone-marrow donor.
- You may be called on to volunteer your time or donate money and material goods to a worthy cause.
- You may be moved to smile at someone on the street and change the course of his or her day, or life.
- You may find yourself looking upon another, for the first time in his or her experience, without judgment, just love and understanding.

When such an opportunity is placed before you, remember to show your gratitude by saying thank you to God and your Angels and Guides. Gratitude is an integral part of the soul-growth process.

SIMPLE HUMAN TRUTH

Angels are always waiting in the wings to assist us on our journey through this life. ALWAYS.

Missing a Spiritual Sign

The types of spiritual signs the Universe will place before us will be perfectly designed for optimal learning on that day or in that moment in time. If a day goes by and we don't find a person to help, it could be because we missed the sign, or pushed it away. In any case, we must not grow complacent and we must continue to *want* to see the signs and act upon them when we do. This next story demonstrates the importance of being on the lookout for spiritual signs and the learning opportunities contained within each experience.

I was on my way to show a real estate client a house on the other side of town and was running late. As I came flying down the highway off-ramp before stopping at the corner, I saw in front of me a man holding a sign asking for money. Judgment about this man came bubbling up as I sat waiting for my light to turn green.

"Get a job," I thought.

As I drove away, I quickly realized my error and blurted out loud, "That was the person I had the opportunity to help today!"

I immediately got back on the highway to turn around so I could face my opportunity for the second time. It couldn't have been but three to five minutes before I flew down the off ramp again, by now running extremely late to my appointment. I approached the same corner where the man had stood moments before, but he was gone. He must have packed up right after I drove by him the first time. I had missed my opportunity.

As I drove away a thought popped into my head: "What if the opportunity for that encounter was two-fold?" I pondered. "What if I was supposed to show that man compassion and kindness, and learn to release judgment regarding another soul's journey?

What if *his* lesson was to learn about patience, or how God works through the hearts of others when you may least expect it?"

The more I thought about this two-fold lesson concept, the more I knew it to be simply true.

SIMPLE HUMAN TRUTH
The Universe places opportunities in each person's path to assist our souls in some way. It is our choice to see the opportunity placed before us, or to go out and find it.

Trusting My Gut, Saving a Life

A Spiritual Samaritan learns how to tap into what feels right, using his or her gut intuition on a moment's notice. Sometimes this means overriding the logical mind to assist another in some big or small way, or even to save the life of one or many souls.

The story doesn't end with the souls saved or assisted that day; these souls may in turn change or save the lives of other souls as the story is shared, inspiring others to do the same. Miracles happen in the lives of others with the extension of our positive and loving energy.

For example, ten years ago I was a passenger in a car coming home from a movie, traveling down a Minnesota country road at dusk after a sweltering summer day. I had been looking straight ahead at the road before me when something blue in my peripheral vision caught my attention. We kept driving until a feeling of panic swept over me.

Without warning I started to chant, "Turn around, turn around, turn around!"

The driver of the car looked at me as if I had just landed on earth from Venus. He finally relented, if only to quiet the chatter from the passenger seat. We turned around and approached the point in the road where I had seen a flash of blue moments before. As we closed in on the spot, I swung the door open and jumped out before the car even came to a complete stop. Lying down in a ditch was a man in a blue T-shirt. I ran back to the car shouting, "Call 9-1-1! Call 9-1-1!"

I returned to the man and touched his shoulder. "Are you with me?" I said. "Please, please, are you with me?"

He cried out in pain, "My back. My back."

I said, "Help is on the way. Just hang in there with me." I wanted him to know he was not alone, that we were now a team and I would not leave him until help had arrived.

By the time the paramedics arrived on the scene it was nearly dark. The man told us that he must have passed out while walking in the heat of the day and rolled into the ditch below. As she administered life-saving IV fluids, the female paramedic informed the man that his kidneys were shutting down from dehydration, and that this was the cause of his severe back pain.

She then turned to me and said, "It's almost dark. Thank goodness you found him when you did. He would have been gone in another hour or two."

Listening to our inner voice can save our life or that of another. That means doing what feels right in our gut, even when everyone or everything is telling us to do something else. Many times there is no time to wait for someone else to come and save the day. *You* might be the one the Universe chooses to put in a specific place at a specific moment to create a miracle.

When you are blessed with the opportunity to save the life of another soul (or creature), you receive a moment in time so sacred it affords you the unique chance to realize these very important things:

- Each and every life is incredibly precious, including yours.
- The Universe is powerful indeed to be able to create the alignments that place us in each other's paths.
- We are capable of far greater things than we choose to believe.

Remember to look at all the factors in each situation—do not blindly leap into danger. If it's safe to do so and it feels right in your gut, then go forth with confidence and become the earthly Angel that saves a soul.

SIMPLE HUMAN TRUTH

Listening to our inner voice can save our life or that of another. That means doing what feels right in our gut, even when everyone or everything is telling us to do something else.

Touched by an Angel in the City of Angels

"Trina," Molly's Guardian Angel by Angel artist Paulette Salo

Sometimes the person in need of assistance is you, and if no earthly Angel is available and it is within Divine Order, other forces called Guardian Angels can intervene from the heavens.

It was a beautiful sunny day in Los Angeles, where I was then living as a carefree young adult. My friend Don, whom I met shortly after arriving in the city, had borrowed a motorcycle from a friend and wanted to know if I would like to join him for a ride. He could feel my apprehension and assured me that we would be safe by staying on the side streets instead of traveling on the busy L.A. freeway. That simple explanation sounded good to me, so we hopped on the motorcycle with confidence but without helmets. On the return trip to my apartment, we were both feeling more confident than ever about Don's motorcycle skills and decided to take the freeway instead of the slower, safer side streets. Within moments we were heading down the freeway entrance ramp at 50 mph. Don miscalculated his speed, however, and as we approached the bottom of the ramp the front tire of the motorcycle hit the cement curb. The moment the tire hit the obstruction, everything began moving in slow motion except my mind. Thoughts flooded and flowed through it at lightning speed. I remember thinking: "I haven't been out here very long...I can't believe I'm not wearing a helmet." My final flashing thought as I was bounced off the back of the motorcycle was, "What will my parents do for my funeral?"

At that moment my hands instinctively grabbed Don's shirt and then his shoulders; they were now the only point of contact I had with Don and the motorcycle. It was at this time—and there was no mistaking it—I felt something from above physically push me back down onto the bike. I didn't realize it at the time, but I do now. It was the gift of life from my Guardian Angel. I landed on the seat just as Don regained control. We pulled over to the side of the highway, both shaken up and in a state of shock but, thank heavens, safe.

Some people live through their mistakes and some don't. Every fragment of time we experience here on earth in our lives is divinely orchestrated, and that moment in time was not designated as my time to be injured or leave this earth unexpectedly. Our personal Guardian Angel travels with us from the moment of our births. Guardian Angels can intervene to save a life if it is not yet Divine Time for a life to end. Living by understanding Divine Reason and Divine Timing can bring us peace and understanding through difficult circumstances.

SIMPLE HUMAN TRUTH
Guardian Angels can intervene to save a life if it is not yet Divine Time for a soul to leave this earth.

Showing Gratitude for an Earlier Blessing

Three years after my Guardian Angel encounter on the back of a motorcycle, the Universe presented me with a synchronistic and eerily similar opportunity to return the favor to a soul on earth.

It was very late at night and I was very pregnant. I lived in an apartment building at the end of a large, circular, manmade lake called Silverlake Reservoir. It was common for people to speed past the reservoir and then underestimate the sharpness of the turn as they came around the corner right in front of my building. I had just opened the window that faced the street when I heard a horrible crash. I looked out and couldn't believe what I was seeing. Down on the street below lay a motorcycle on its side and two motionless bodies. The riders, both without helmets, had come around the corner too fast and had wiped out, hitting their heads on the unforgiving cement street.

I stood in shock, looking out my window until a feeling of urgency came over me. I heard a voice in my head say, "Get out there right now!" Everything once again played out in slow

45

motion except the words that came out of my mouth: "What are you doing?" Followed by, "Get out there!"

I overrode my logical mind, which was telling me to be sensible, to "stay put and call 9-1-1," that someone else would take care of it. I shook my head to clear my thoughts and decided to listen to the voice. I snapped into action and ran out to the street.

I had been out there for less than a minute when I could see a car's headlights bouncing off the road in our direction. I ran up ahead to stop the car before it ran over the accident victims around the corner. The man I flagged down drove an old VW bus. He was a kind soul and immediately pulled his vehicle sideways, blocking traffic to prevent any future catastrophe. More people who'd heard the crash arrived on the scene. The man that drove the VW bus yelled, "Someone call 9-1-1!"

With our blockade in place, we rushed back to the young man and woman lying unconscious in the street. I said a prayer in my head: "God, please may these people be all right." As the ambulance drivers arrived and loaded the two injured motorcyclists into separate ambulances, each one began to moan. I never did find out what happened to that motorcyclist and his companion that night, but I do know this: The magnificent Universe places events in front of us that are divinely orchestrated and synchronistic such that it becomes almost impossible for the ego to refute this fact: Forces much bigger than us are guiding everything behind the scenes.

As I look back at events in my life, like the one I just mentioned, I see that each one has a specific meaning, and each has taught me the lessons that have allowed me to arrive at the place I am today.

SIMPLE HUMAN TRUTH

*The magnificent Universe places events in front of us
that are divinely orchestrated and synchronistic such that
it becomes almost impossible for the ego to refute this fact:
Forces much bigger than us are guiding everything
behind the scenes.*

Angels at the Airport

Sometimes the simple lesson placed before us to grow our souls is not so much about helping another on a moment's notice but about asking for help on our own behalf!

My husband Peter and I love each other's companionship and many times when he travels out of town on business I'll tag along. One time Peter and I were at the Minneapolis airport, heading to San Diego for a trade show. I have never been fond of X-ray technology, so instead of going through the full body-scanning machine at the security gate, I had opted for an invigorating full-body pat down. The security personnel instructed me to remove everything from my pockets, including my driver's license, which I hurriedly put in my zipperless jacket pocket and placed in the plastic bin before me. After I was cleared to go through security, I grabbed my jacket, tied it around my waist, and headed to our gate after making a pit stop at the restroom. I joined my husband just as our flight was being called and instinctively reached for my driver's license in my pocket. A flush went through me as I realized it was gone.

As I retraced my steps in my mind, I put out an immediate "all call" to my Angel and Guide team: "Angels and Guides, I need your help. Please find my driver's license, thank you." Meanwhile, Peter headed back to "Checkpoint Charlie" to see if the license was left behind in the plastic bin.

Moments later, a woman's voice boomed over the loudspeaker. "Molly Friedenfeld, please come to the counter for your identification." I looked up. My heart fluttered with joy as I realized some Spiritual Samaritan must have turned in my license.

"Which counter should I go to, Angels?" I asked as I scanned the five counters in the gate area and approached the one that felt right. "I am Molly Friedenfeld." I announced. "Did you happen to find my driver's license?"

The counter person handed over my license. I held it up to the heavens and said, "Thank you, thank you, thank you!"

Synchronistic Reciprocity

As I've stated before, each moment is divinely orchestrated and divinely guided. There is nothing that happens without reason. When we receive a blessing, the Universe often presents us with a follow-up opportunity to bless someone in return. Grasp every such opportunity as it comes along by graciously blessing another human, the planet, or one of God's creatures.

Four months after temporarily losing my license at the Minneapolis airport, I was given this chance. As I was getting out of my car at the local shopping mall, I looked down to find a woman's driver's license and credit card on the ground by the car next to mine. I smiled and said, "Thank you, Angels!"

I finished my shopping that day and returned home to try and locate a phone number for the woman whose name appeared on the driver's license. My search came up empty and I resorted to mailing the license to the address located on the ID. Inside the envelope with the license and credit card I included my business card with a short note on the back letting her know where I found the items.

One week later, the woman called and left a sincere voicemail message. She said her name was Lillian and that she was currently traveling out of state on business but had just received her license in the mail, forwarded on by her husband. She went on to say that in order to travel, she had resorted to using her passport as airport ID, and wanted to thank me personally for being so honest.

SIMPLE HUMAN TRUTH
Each moment is divinely orchestrated and divinely guided. There is nothing that happens without reason. When we receive a blessing, the Universe often presents us with a follow-up opportunity to bless someone in return. Grasp every such opportunity as it comes along by graciously blessing another human, the planet, or one of God's creatures.

Angels and Spirit Guides

We all have a mission. We all have a purpose. Our personal Angels and Spirit Guides travel alongside us to guide us and assist us in fulfilling all the things our *pure* hearts desire. We have armies of Angels at our disposal. These lovely beings can help us bring Heaven to earth so all of us can experience a peaceful and joyful journey during our designated time here.

It is our personal choice whether to seek Divine Guidance and assistance as we travel through our days and along our personal journeys, or to venture into the unknown alone. We know now that in order for Angels and Guides to help us with a specific request, we must make an active choice to acknowledge them and grant them permission by asking for their assistance. The more we talk to them, the more we will feel their heavenly energy surround us. And the more we feel their presence, the more we understand that we are all divinely connected. Awareness of this connection is what drives each Spiritual Samaritan to reach out with love to as many souls as possible, thus becoming a heart-centered earthly Angel.

Angel and Spirit Guide Communication Challenge:

For one week, I challenge you to BELIEVE. All you have to do is say, "I believe in Angels and Guides" and be ready and open to receive their spiritual signs. These signs may come in the form of symbols, song lyrics, scriptures, commercials, or words spoken by another in conversation. The number of possible spiritual signs they will flow to you to prove their existence is immeasurable. Have fun!

Specific signs from Angel and Spirit Guides may include:

- Seeing an Angel statue or Angel pin
- Finding pennies, dimes, and feathers in random locations
- Hearing a song lyric mentioning the word *Angel*
- Picking up a book that speaks of Angels
- Having a friend comment, "You are an Angel."
- Running across the name Angel, Angela, or Raphael on a license plate
- Seeing a halo in a store window
- Seeing an Angel on a billboard or in a magazine or newspaper article
- Waking up from a vivid dream involving Angels
- Seeing an Angel tattoo

Here are some easy steps for communicating directly with Angels and Spirit Guides:

- Become centered with love in your heart space.
- Say, "Please," and ask your Angels and Guides what you desire to see as a specific form of communication. Use your imagination and ask them for unique signs that prove they are real. For example, ask to see a purple horse, a crown, barbed wire, Angel wings, or even a three-legged dog!
- Say, "Thank you" and "I BELIEVE."
- Release the request to the Universe. You must actually *believe* that it will occur in order to stay in alignment (on track) for receiving your sign.
- Allow your Angels and Guides to work behind the scenes to flow your sign to you and be on the lookout for it!
- When you see your sign, be sure to say, "Thank you" to show your gratitude.

SIMPLE HUMAN TRUTH
When Angels whisper in your ear, it is your heart that hears their message.

Soul Food and Illumination

You can help another believe in heavenly Angels by becoming an earthly Angel yourself. Back in 2007, I met a man named Mike via a real estate referral. Mike became one of my favorite clients, but more importantly, he became one of my good friends. He was the kind of client real-estate agents dream about. He knew exactly the type of house he wanted, and we found it on the first day we went out looking. Moreover, he was a kind and gentle soul with a great sense of humor. He would constantly pay forward his gratitude to me for finding his dream home so quickly by introducing me as "Molly, my favorite Realtor." I would correct him each time by jokingly stating, "Mike had only one Realtor, so it was pretty easy to become his favorite."

Mike was also a man of immense character and integrity, with a heart of gold. He opened his heart and his home to all. He loved to invite his children and their friends over for big, family-style meals. He was a true professional at filling youthful stomachs with comfort food.

Mike also touched the hearts of those that needed it most with kind actions and words. For example, each Christmas, Mike's front yard looked like a scene from the movie *National Lampoon's Christmas Vacation*. He hung twinkling lights from every branch of the trees in his yard and adorned every square inch of the front of his home with decorations. When I asked him, "Why do you go to all this effort every year?" He simply stated, "It makes me happy and I like bringing people in the neighborhood together."

In 2010, the earthly Angel named Mike was called home unexpectedly, but not before leaving his mark on many hearts in this world, including mine. My friend Mike taught me how to demonstrate love to others unconditionally by lighting up our world in many unique ways. He also taught me that connecting with the heart of another comes through many different avenues, including the stomach.

An earthly Angel that changes lives with food is called a "food Fairy" or "food Angel." This is a person who feeds the heart by way of the stomach through heart-centered cooking, or "soul food."

RECIPE FOR A CUP OF CHEER
AT ANY TIME OF YEAR...
1 tsp. Kindness
1 tsp. Peace
1 tsp. Joy
1 tsp. Compassion
1 tsp. Love
1 tsp. Gratitude
Combine, then serve to those around
you with a giving heart.

Go Forth and Make It Happen

Ordinary humans become soul-centered earthly Angels like Mike while walking this earth by loving others unconditionally and spreading peace, joy, and kindness with a magical touch. That is what it really means to be a Spiritual Samaritan: We are everyday advocates, motivating others and touching lives in ways we may never have thought possible.

Here are some ideas for doing just that:

- **Become a difference maker.** Start the day with a simple prayer asking God, Angels, Guides—whatever you call your Higher Power—to put someone in front of you that you can assist in some big or small way so that you can become a Spiritual Samaritan/earthly Angel. Then watch what happens!

- **Show gratitude.** When you receive a blessing, the Universe always presents a follow-up opportunity to bless someone in return. Grasp every opportunity for gratitude as it comes along by graciously blessing another human, the planet, or one of God's creatures.

- **Teach it forward.** If you have gathered great wisdom through a difficult lesson, tell others about it. By telling your story honestly, with humility, and from your heart, you can give others insight regarding a problem they may be experiencing and become the instrument for another soul's learning and growth.
- **Demonstrate it.** Show others the way by being a positive role model and demonstrating how becoming a Spiritual Samaritan/earthly Angel blesses the lives of all those that come across our path.

The Gracious Samaritan

When encountering a Spiritual Samaritan, such as a volunteer in the community or anyone performing a good deed, acknowledge that person with heartfelt gratitude. Extending gratitude to another says, "I see what you've done and I thank you for the energy you put forth." Showing gratitude toward another is simple and always poignant. We can all reflect back on situations when we remember the effect of kind words in our lives.

Gratitude brings value to any situation. When a person receives a compliment, a pat on the back, or some form of recognition, he or she is immediately bathed in a moment of warmth and love. This process of extending gracious gratitude feeds all souls involved—the giver and the receiver—and is a catalyst that keeps love in motion. Gratitude can be the element that *becomes a day-changer* for one and *saves the life* of another.

SIMPLE HUMAN TRUTH

Extending gratitude to another says, "I see what you've done and I thank you for the energy you put forth."

Pay It Forward

A purposeful act or extension of kindness to another is never wasted, for it always resides in the hearts of all involved in a chain of love. The 2000 movie *Pay it Forward*, starring Kevin Spacey and Haley Joel Osment, demonstrated the powerful ripple effect that occurs when we extend ourselves to another soul unconditionally.

In 2011, my mother decided to have a *Pay it Forward* type of Christmas. She wanted to make a difference in the lives of others by having each family member start our own chain of making a difference. So instead of presents that might be returned or exchanged, she gave all of her kids, grandkids, and great-grandkids a card with a ten-dollar bill inside. She asked that each of us take the ten dollars and give it away to one person, or more than one person, in need. That meant we could give it all to one person, one dollar each to ten people, and so on. All she asked for in return was the story behind the giving.

My husband, Peter, and I donated our money to an animal shelter that rescues ill and injured animals. Our daughter Maddy donated her money to a fundraiser to benefit a woman with cancer. Our other daughter, Mallory, and granddaughter, Hailey, donated their money to an organization that helps wounded soldiers. Each donation was unique, showing the beautifully diverse and immense possibilities for becoming Spiritual Samaritans.

SIMPLE HUMAN TRUTH
A purposeful act or extension of kindness to another is never wasted, for it always resides in the hearts of all involved in a chain of love.

Pray It Forward

This next story shows why earthly Angels never exclude souls from their Divine Intentions. When we begin to see that we are part of a bigger picture of connectedness, it becomes easier to understand why prayer and forgiveness heal everyone involved: the victim, the perpetrator, and all the souls left behind, including the one praying.

Roberta Elam was a twenty-six-year-old adult religious education teacher who planned to join Wheeling, West Virginia's Sisters of St. Joseph. On June 13, 1977, she grabbed her Bible and an apple from the kitchen and headed to the hill behind the convent to pray. Later, a caretaker found Roberta's body behind an overturned bench. She had been brutally raped and strangled. The murder case remains unsolved to this day.

About fifteen years later, cold-case detectives took two psychics separately out to the crime scene where the stone bench was located. The investigators had asked the psychics to see if they could read the energy there and pick up any information that would help them with the unsolved case. Each psychic reported, "I don't feel anything here but love, just pure love."

The investigators were stumped as to why the psychics weren't picking up the violent energy they expected, or any details from the crime that had occurred there. When the investigators walked back to the convent, the nuns told them that every morning and evening since the crime occurred, they had gone up the hill and prayed at that precise location. They pray for the woman who lost her life there, and for the man who took her life.

The bad energy from this horrific event has been wiped clean through prayer by the energy of God's healing, for not a trace of hatred or violence remains, only love.

SIMPLE HUMAN TRUTH

When we begin to see that we are part of a bigger picture of connectedness, it becomes easier to understand why prayer and forgiveness heal everyone involved: the victim, the perpetrator, and all the souls left behind, including the one praying.

Making a Difference with Prayer

As the above story demonstrates, it's easy to pray for those we love, but it is just as important to pray for those people that cause us the most pain and difficulty and to forgive them. The act of praying for another who has caused us discomfort takes us away from the location of victimization, which exists only in our mind, and allows us to learn as we forgive, this moves us to the location of peace, which resides deep within our hearts, causing a shift in our souls.

Here is how to say intentional prayers of love, forgiveness, and learning:

- Close your eyes.
- Sit with your feet on the floor.

- Take several deep breaths in and out to calm yourself and focus your mind.
- Hold the person you need to forgive in your mind's eye.
- Imagine encircling the person completely in a clear bubble of energy and bring God's beautiful white light straight down from the heavens, allowing the light to fill the entire bubble.
- Repeat the process, sending down green healing light from the heavens to fill the bubble.
- Begin sending him or her thoughts of healing, love, and forgiveness, followed by loving energy straight from your pure heart.
- Recite the prayer(s) below.
- When you are finished, thank God for His grace and open your eyes.

FIRST PRAYER:

God, please soften my heart so that I may pray for (name specific person[s]), who has hurt me. I am hoping to find peace and forgiveness in this process. I also pray that you would soften the hearts of those whom I may have wronged so that they may in turn be prompted to do the same for me, and that all of our souls receive forgiveness. Amen.

SECOND PRAYER:

God, I thank you for softening my heart. I pray that you and your heavenly Angels and Guides would take my hand and guide me down the correct path and reveal to me the lessons behind the event(s) that have caused me great pain with (name specific person[s]). I am ready for the lesson to be revealed and open to finding the answers put before me so that I may further my soul's growth. God, please forgive (name specific person[s]) for the wrong that has been done to me. I ask now that you would fill each of our hearts with your love and healing light. Amen.

SIMPLE HUMAN TRUTH

It's easy to pray for those we love, but it is just as important to pray for those people that cause us the most pain and difficulty and to forgive them.

Speed Praying

My sister Carolyn called me one afternoon in early February 2012. Her voice sounded anguished, and she got right to the point: "We need immediate prayers! There is a young man getting ready to jump off the bridge in Anoka. I just drove by him." She explained, "There are three cars stopped in the street. One man is on a cell phone and there are people trying to talk him down."

I immediately stopped what I was doing and imagined bringing beautiful white light down from the heavens and encircling this man in God's unconditional love so he could feel the connection to Source. I then asked my Angels to go find this man's Angels so they could help guide him to safety. I then imagined this man's personal Angels gliding in and gently wrapping him in their expansive wings and saw the Angels placing him into the loving arms of the Spiritual Samaritans on the bridge who were helping him that day.

Days later, I looked online for more information about this event and could not find any mention of it. I took this as a good sign, for today it seems our news media have a tendency to report only bad news, and perhaps a story that didn't end in tragedy was not newsworthy enough to make headlines.

I am so thankful that Carolyn, my Spiritual Samaritan sister, took the time to put out an all-call for assistance that day. Have faith in knowing that even if an event may end in the unexpected or untimely death of another, there is still a blessing for that soul and all souls involved when people come together with love and prayer. If someone you know may have committed suicide, died an untimely death, or even left this earth with a hardened heart, then pray, pray, pray. Loving prayer is powerful. All souls, even those on the other side, benefit.

What Carolyn and I did that day was *speed praying*. Speed praying is the simple act of sending love, healing, and prayer for yourself or another.

Speed praying is a simple healing tool:

- Speed praying is appropriate anywhere, at any time, and in any circumstance.
- You can speed pray with many people at once using Facebook, Twitter, or texting. Start a speed prayer group. When the need appears, you can send a message in moments to multiple recipients. It's that simple.
- Speed praying can also be utilized when you feel tempted in any way. Perhaps you are in the process of conquering some kind of addiction or personal challenge. Put out an all-call to friends, family, and those you trust to speed pray for you to help you feel strongly connected during times of need.

SIMPLE HUMAN TRUTH

Have faith in knowing that even if an event may end in the unexpected or untimely death of another, there is still a blessing for that soul and all souls involved when people come together with love and prayer.

Peace, Joy, and Faith

If you know someone who has given up hope, try giving that person some of your peace, joy, and faith! By being a person who lives with peace, joy, and faith in your heart, you serve as an earthly Angel who allows others to feel grounded, loved, and needed when they are in your presence. You can be the person who lets other souls know they are worthy. You can be the beacon that lights up a dark day and guides a soul over the bridge that carries him or her over turbulent waters during difficult times. You can be the difference maker who starts a compassionate project in your community that brings people closer together. And finally, you can be the one person in someone's life who honestly says, "Stick in there. I have faith in you. You can do it!"

When a person experiences receiving someone's complete faith in him or her, or is part of a movement that has unconditional love as its foundation, that person is motivated to move into a more conscious, soul-centered, and faith-filled state of being.

SIMPLE HUMAN TRUTH

If you know someone that has given up hope, try giving that person some of your peace, joy, and faith!

* * *

Finding and maintaining our sense of inner peace and then giving it away in the form of unconditional love allows us to share our hearts with others. Another important element in the soul-growth process is joy. In order to consistently maintain a state of joy, we need to "befriend" our emotions. Any time our emotions have shifted in a negative direction, those emotions allow us to illuminate that we are out of alignment. This emotional truth, in turn, allows us to realize we need to shift ourselves back to the positive—peace and joy—as quickly as possible. Staying in a state of peace and joy means we are consciously checking in with our emotions throughout our days. This next chapter will show you how to do this.

Joy

SPREADING SUNSHINE

The entire time I was painting this image, the vibration that, to me, indicates Molly's mother was pulsing full blast in my being. I could even see her in the image that was coming through. She is one of a multitude focused on elevating all human hearts to the joy frequency and often comes through to Molly in the form of yellow: yellow butterflies, yellow cars, yellow everything. Why wouldn't she show up to spread sunshine by adding her high frequency of joy to Molly's book? Here she is kicking around sunshine, spreading the light of love and joy.

Spreading Sunshine

Spend as much time as possible with positive, joyful people and as little time as possible with negative, unhappy people.

Finding Joy on the Journey

In October 2011, during an impromptu spiritual reading session with my friend Michelle Beltran, my father came through with a message for me to get started writing a book—this one. During that reading I remember being flabbergasted.

Through Michelle, I told him, "I'm not a writer. I'm a real estate agent." His message in return was short and sweet.

He replied, "It doesn't matter. You have everything. Get going."

My father loved to use the phrase "get going," as his short and to-the-point message of motivation. He never resorted to long, drawn-out speeches, so I knew in my gut this message was from him, exactly as he would have delivered it.

One month later, I met a woman named Cynthia Shepherd at a local spiritual fair. CJ, as people like to call her, is now one of my closest friends. I find it truly wonderful how people get placed before you at the precise moment you need to meet them. As I've mentioned, life is full of these fabulous synchronistic events once you start to look for the meaning behind seemingly chance encounters.

That day, I decided to have a reading with CJ. I wanted to see if, without any prompting, she could connect with my father and provide me with more information about this book that I was supposed to write. During that reading she did connect with him and he confirmed once again, through CJ, that I was in fact supposed to be writing a book. It was a predestined purpose my soul set in place for me to accomplish in this lifetime.

I also received the message that in order to get started on the book, I had a lot of work to do on myself first. I needed to enjoy the spiritual awakening process I was experiencing right now, and equally important, I needed to practice patience, for the rest would be presented to me in Divine Order.

I now had confirmation about the book I was supposed to write from two separate people who didn't know my father, or each other, but who had each clearly identified only things my father would know or say as validation—and both came up with the same message.

Many of the things I was experiencing, learning, and hearing from others I believed in my heart and embraced. The things I hadn't been embracing were patience and joy. I was determined to learn all this spiritual stuff quickly, at my pace and on my own controlled terms. However, this is not how the Universe works. Gaining wisdom is not a race against time. Everything is divinely guided and revealed when we are ready for it, and not one moment before, no matter how much we whine, cry, complain, or how quickly we *think* we are learning.

I had one more reading at the fair that day by a man named Bobby Sullivan. Bobby is an intuitive energy worker. He uses a machine with a light-sensitive camera to read the energy of your aura. The camera takes a picture of your energy field and shoots out a Polaroid picture. Once it develops, he gives you a reading based on the information he receives while tapping into your energy field and looking at the specific colors that have developed on the photo.

My reading with Bobby produced another message of reinforcement. He told me that the aura photo showed I was taking everything way too seriously. He said nonchalantly, "Lighten up. Don't take everything so personally." He went on to say, "It is very important for you to work on yourself first and grow your own spirit before you can effectively help others, so enjoy the ride in order to get where you ultimately want to go."

Instead of feeling gratitude for the "themed" messages containing immense wisdom that the spiritual readers had dispensed to grow my spirit, I left those sessions with a very heavy heart. I did the opposite of what I was told and took it personally. I left the building and went out to my car and cried like a baby. Once I had successfully cried off all my makeup, I regained my composure as most of us do by stuffing the remainder of my emotions inward, putting the key in the ignition, and driving away.

I was a few miles down the road when I remembered that my friend Lisa, a fellow real estate agent, had asked me to pick up some white sage from a Tibetan store down the street from the spiritual fair. Lisa liked to use white sage to clear a house of any negative energy before listing it for sale. I kept driving, though, until the thought about picking up the white sage returned with a message attached. This time it didn't just pop into my head; it came in with a noticeable *thump,* followed by the words, "Turn around!"

"Hello Dad." I said.

Here he was again, guiding me with unconditional (and no-nonsense) love from the other side. I reluctantly did what I was told, turned around, wiped the tears off my face, and reached

THE BOOK OF SIMPLE HUMAN TRUTHS

for my lipstick. Why? Because for some foolish reason I thought applying something of a different shade to my lips would take the focus off the fact that just moments before I was bawling my eyes out. Quite silly, I know.

Minutes later I pulled up in front of a little Tibetan store located in a quaint suburb of Minneapolis called Linden Hills. I got out of my car and dragged myself to the door. As I opened it, the metal bells signaling a new customer clanked above my head. After the storeowner finished assisting two customers, who then left, he turned his attention to me.

"What do you need?" he asked.

I said. "I am here to pick up some white sage for my friend."

He said. "We do not have white sage here, but what do you need?"

I replied. "That's all I came in for, but thank you."

I think he could sense that I was ready to bolt toward the door, so he got right to the point. "Why are you so sad? You have no joy in your heart."

I thought to myself. "Seriously, I just put on lipstick to keep people off the track that I was just bawling my eyes out. Man, this Tibetan dude is perceptive." My eyes immediately began welling up with tears.

He walked right past me, reached into a glass case, and pulled out a very old gold bowl with a mallet inside it and said, "Stand right there."

I did as I was told, all the while wondering what the heck this had to do with the white sage I had initially come in for.

I could hear him swirling the mallet around in the bowl behind my head, and then even more swirling, until my ears rang with the final sounds from the side of the bowl. *Bing! Bang! Bong!* The shopkeeper put the bowl on the counter, looked me in the eyes, and said, "You must find your own joy before you can help others."

I couldn't believe what I was hearing: another message so similar to the one I had received from Bobby and CJ's spiritual readings just thirty minutes before. I knew this was no coincidence. This was Universal Wisdom coming through once again, this time via a repetitive theme, leaving no chance of my not receiving the message loud and clear.

The kind Tibetan man now had my full attention. He pointed to my head and then my heart. "You must move from your head down to your heart. Find the joy in your heart first, then you will be able to help others."

I felt for a moment like The Karate Kid receiving ancient wisdom from Mr. Miyagi. The shopkeeper picked up the bowl and mallet once again and said, "Now, I want you to meditate. Put yourself on a beautiful beach. Feel the sand beneath your toes. See the clouds in the bright blue sky above, and then feel the joy that resides within you."

I did as I was told. It seemed like an eternity, even though I know it lasted only a minute or two. I never thought of it before, but my mind, up until recently, had never been afforded the luxury of stillness via any form of meditation allowing for simple solitude for more than thirty seconds during my waking hours.

I focused on the beach scene, as instructed. As I did so I imagined writing the word JOY across the bright blue sky with a make-believe white crayon to make this vision more interactive. As I wrote the words, they turned into fluffy white clouds that expanded and traveled effortlessly across my mind's eye. I took a deep breath in and a deep breath out. I felt lighter. Happier. I felt something shift in me.

The mallet hit the side of the bowl again. *Bing! Bang! Bong!*

The Tibetan man kindly commanded, "Now, open your eyes." I began to slowly open my eyes. Standing before me, he said, "It's very important to meditate in joy for five minutes every day." He reiterated: "Once you find this joy within you, then you will be able to effectively help others."

He gave me a hug like a father gives his daughter, and at the same time I felt it was the kind of hug we most likely receive when Angels greet us in Heaven—welcoming, healing, and loving.

I wiped the tears from my eyes and said, "Thank you for the healing." As the last word left my mouth the bells above the door clanked, signaling the arrival of four people entering the store. I knew then that my Divine Healing session was over.

The Universe continued to send me signs in the days following to reinforce my lessons about the importance of living with joy in my heart. On one particular occasion, my husband Peter and I decided to go on a long walk around the marsh area by our home in Minneapolis. We weren't on the walk for more than a few minutes when we saw a man and his young daughter approaching with their dog. The two were skipping. They were having so much fun, and their joy was contagious. My husband and I smiled as they skipped past us. I actually giggled it was so cute. They were living with joy in their hearts and demonstrating it to others.

"I'll do the same." I thought to myself. *"I will remember to do the same."*

I had finally acknowledged and openly received my themed lessons from the Universe.

We must all be able to find our way to joy while consistently working on our soul's growth. Joy is the personal cheerleader that can keep us skipping along during down periods. In order to experience joy, we must move from our heads and learn to live from our heart space. Once we arrive at this warm location, our compassionate heart expands and we begin to find new and joyful ways to extend ourselves effectively to others unconditionally.

SIMPLE HUMAN TRUTH

In order to experience joy, we must move from our heads and learn to live from our heart space. Once we arrive at this warm location, our compassionate heart expands and we begin to find new and joyful ways to extend ourselves effectively to others unconditionally.

Lemon Drops

Finding our joy is one of the main reasons we are here on this planet. We know when we have manifested and reached a place of joy, because whatever it is we are doing at that moment, our hearts are singing. We are completely present. We are *enjoying* ourselves. This state of being means we are in *alignment* or in a positive *vibration location*. Alignment means we are on the right track, and a vibration location is an energetic place.

If we are driving a car that is out of alignment and take our hands off the steering wheel, the car will begin to veer left or right and eventually go right off the road. The same applies to humans. If we are out of alignment with peace and joy, we may embrace the negative, placing us in a negative vibration location. Thus, we may veer off the road—our spiritual path—and into a metaphorical ditch. We then can become stuck in this new negative place in our minds, plagued with looping thoughts, engaging in drama, blaming others, and constant complaining. If the car we are driving is in alignment, we continue to move ahead straight for some distance, even if we take our hands off the wheel, remaining in a positive vibration location of peace and joy. This state allows all the wonderful things the Universe has to offer us to flow right in.

If you are feeling down and want to return to the alignment of joy, quickly imagine popping a lemon drop in your mouth. Notice how it fills you with instant sunshine inside, bringing you back into joyful alignment.

One may say, "It's not possible to be in *joy* all the time. How are you going to find joy if someone is dying?" Yet, we can actually find our way to joy while sitting next to the bed of a soul who is terminally ill or days from crossing over to God's light. How do we accomplish this? We can feel joy by appreciating every single moment we have with that person before his or her spirit leaves the physical body, and then, after the transition, be grateful for every intentional moment we had and the memories we created.

Another example of appropriate joy in the midst of sadness can be found in a scene from the movie *Life is Beautiful* starring joyful actor/director Roberto Benigni. In one of the most poignant scenes, Benigni's character, Guido, is being led around the corner of a building to be shot by the Nazis as his young son watches. Instead of crying, screaming, and carrying on, Guido finds his joy even in the moments before his death. With a huge smile on his face, he pretends he is a soldier marching in a funny parade. Why? Because he wants his son to know that life is beautiful.

Joy brings meaning and purpose to our lives:

- Joy enhances all life experiences.
- Joy is looking at every person in your life as a pure blessing because each one is an Illuminator, helping you to shed light on the truth and feel and experience many different emotions to further your soul's growth.

- Joy is the feeling of facing a life lesson head on with gratitude and acceptance.

SIMPLE HUMAN TRUTH

If you are feeling down, imagine popping a lemon drop in your mouth. It fills you with instant sunshine inside.

Smile

I once had a real estate client named Jenna. She worked in downtown Minneapolis and had such a great attitude. We liked to share positive life stories as we drove around together looking for that perfect house. One day she said, "Molly, do you know what I do when I walk through the skyway system on my way to work?"

I replied, "No. What do you do?"

She said, "I smile at people. I don't say anything, I just give them a big smile as I pass by my fellow human."

I questioned, "What do people do in return?"

She responded, "Some look very confused. I can tell that in their heads they are thinking, is she smiling at me? *Why* is she smiling at me?" She went on, "I can tell that for some people, it really touches their hearts. My simple smile makes them feel good, and it makes me feel good. That's precisely why I do it."

Bringing joy to another unconditionally makes our hearts sing and our souls sing louder!

There are many things joy can accomplish:

- Joy creates more joy.
- Joy builds within us as we continue to work on ourselves.

- Your joy can be the impetus that motivates others to find their way to joy.
- Joy allows you to feel and acknowledge all things wonderful while you are on your journey.

SIMPLE HUMAN TRUTH
Your joy can be the impetus that motivates others to find their way to joy.

Truth Brings Joy

If at any time you notice you are not enjoying your life, check in with your emotional feeling center—your gut—and sort through why you are not experiencing joy. There is always a TRUTH to be revealed in any situation where your emotions have shifted. As I mentioned earlier, if your emotions are in a positive vibration location, then you feel great and you know you are on the right track. If your emotions have shifted to the negative vibration location, then you feel bad and you know you are off track; uncovering the truth helps you to recognize immediately why you are out of alignment and what you need to do to bring things back to the positive vibration location.

The moment you notice your feelings shifting from good to bad, start asking questions:

Why am I upset?

What action or thought resulted in the shift?

What do I need to do to shift back to joy?

Once the truth is revealed, acknowledge it and process the emotions surrounding the experience so you can learn and grow.

It is extremely important to release any negative emotions by first recognizing quickly that they have served their purpose to alert you that you are out of alignment and veering off your true path of joy, and then letting them go so you can move forward. Stuffed emotions result in resentment, anxiety, depression, and illness. The more adept you become at working through this process, recognizing each time a shift occurs, the sooner you will be able to return to a joyful state.

SIMPLE HUMAN TRUTH
There is always a TRUTH to be revealed in any situation where your emotions have shifted.

Humor with One Hundred Legs

Not only can truth bring joy, but also joy can transform fear.

Four years ago, I was at my sister Jeannette's house with Mallory and Hailey and Jeannette's two children, Marissa and Mitch. We were watching television in the living room when one of the kids noticed a centipede on the ceiling above the fireplace. The initial reaction of the group was to run out the front door screaming, but instead, we stuck together as a family and became a unified group of screamers. We were like the Three Musketeers, only there were five of us—*One for all and all for one.* All five of us stayed in the room, pointing at the ceiling and screaming.

One of the kids yelled, "Look at how big and juicy that thing is. They have like a hundred legs, you know!"

Someone else screamed, "I think it just hissed at us."

That did it for me. I knew I had to do something quick before

75

the centipede moved across the ceiling, or we would all lose our minds right then and there. I joked, "Marissa and Mitch, if this thing should fall, you will have no other option but to evacuate your home!"

I'm pretty sure it was my niece who came up with the idea to trap the creepy critter under a glass. She didn't want to have to move out of her family home at a young age, which prompted her to be proactive and come up with options for taking care of the incredibly gross situation as quickly as possible.

I took it upon myself to become the "trapper." Once a glass was brought from the kitchen, I lifted it into the air with a shaky hand, screaming all the way, until it reached the ceiling, trapping the centipede. The screams reached airport-engine levels when the centipede fell into the glass and started squirming around inside.

The scream I emitted next came up from my toes as I yelled, "Mitch, go grab something for me to put under this glass! And, for heaven' sake, hurry!"

Mitch returned moments later with a Napoleon Dynamite greeting card. It was one of those musical cards, and when the card was opened so I could slide it under the glass, we heard nerdy Napoleon Dynamite's voice saying, "I have nunchuck skills ... bow hunting skills ... computer hacking skills..."

At that moment, we all stopped screaming and *shifted collectively* to laughter. Once the centipede was safely thrown outside, Napoleon Dynamite greeting card, glass, and all, we reminisced and laughed about our multi-legged encounter. The story of our joy-filled time spent with one creepy centipede has brought us even more joy over the years as one of those *remember when* stories.

At any given time during our life's journey, we get to choose how our stories unfold before us. Choosing the option of working collectively, as a team, brings people together for longer than just that moment, for it allows us to join forces for a cause and in the process create memories. The only thing that keeps us from a place of joy is an illusion, the illusion of fear. Fear is an illusionary place we travel to in our minds when we allow ourselves to move away from the truth. Once we find our way to the truth, we realize we are just fine and only a quick solution may be needed in order to return us to a state of peace and joy. We always have the choice and the power to shift to the positive. We can choose joy over worry. And by the way, choosing joy is way more fun!

SIMPLE HUMAN TRUTH
The only thing that keeps us from a place of joy is an illusion, the illusion of fear.

Joyful Shifting Made Simple

Recognizing we have shifted out of joyful alignment, bringing forth the reason behind the emotional shift as soon as possible by working through the issue, and finally releasing the negativity associated with the shift so we can return to joy is a daily process. Having tools in place to shift you back to joy is an integral part of staying in a joy-filled state of mind.

Shifting can be as simple as:

- Creating a Joy folder on your iPod or music directory containing uplifting music
- Saving kind voicemails, e-mails, or letters for reflection
- Wearing more yellow
- Smiling

- Planting sunflowers or your favorite yellow flower in your garden
- Joining a Laughter Yoga group
- Visiting a comedy club
- Watching uplifting movies and television shows
- Snapping your fingers while saying, "Thank you" to consciously shift your mood back to gratitude
- Doing something for someone else to take the focus off of yourself
- Turning off or avoiding negative news broadcasts, TV shows, magazines, and newspapers
- Spending as much time as possible with positive people and as little time as possible with negative people

Laughter Is the Best Medicine

Did you know the average child laughs hundreds of times a day? The average adult laughs only ten to fifteen. If, as adults, we can have more childlike fun, we learn to enjoy life as it unfolds. Laugh more. Laugh often. Live longer. When we are able to find our personal joy at any moment, we truly begin to live.

The benefits of laughter include:

- Raising your oxygen level
- Snapping you out of the emotional doldrums and returning you to the alignment of joy
- The opportunity to communicate with everyone. Laughter is a universal language.

SIMPLE HUMAN TRUTH
When we are able to find our personal joy at any moment,
we truly begin to live.

Don't Worry. Be Happy

"Keeping our cool" during a stressful situation allows us to demonstrate patience and joy to others. I remember a sweltering hot day in Orlando, Florida when my family and I had just pulled into the lot at the rental-car facility to drop off our car after a fun-filled week at Walt Disney World. Our family pocketbook was drained, but our hearts were filled with great memories as we prepared to depart back to Minneapolis.

I am one of those people who like to try to get to the airport with plenty of time to spare so as to reduce stress while traveling. I've learned from many life-lesson airport experiences that there is nothing that will get me out of my joy alignment faster than running through an airport to catch a plane. I enjoy easing in and easing out of airport experiences whenever I can, so I made sure that we arrived at the rental car facility ahead of schedule.

With the rental car safely in its stall, we boarded the complimentary shuttle bus for the airport. My daughter Mallory, a pre-teen at the time, and I were seated comfortably about half way back from the driver and directly across from a large open space where you could lock up a motorized mobility scooter. As we sat patiently waiting for the rest of the passengers to board the bus, Bobby McFerrin's song, "Don't Worry, Be Happy" (the rental car company's theme song at the time) played over the loudspeakers above our heads. I immediately began humming along and tapping my foot as I reflexively do every time I hear it.

The driver was just getting ready to pull away from the curb when the electric doors of the rental car company's building opened. Out came a woman walking very slowly alongside her husband, a heavyset man riding in a motorized mobility scooter. As they headed toward the bus, Mallory looked at me with panic in her eyes. I could see the wheels turning in her pre-teen brain, thinking something like, "This is going to take forever. I'm going to grow old waiting for these people to board the bus."

I leaned over and sang, "Don't worry. Be happy."

She rolled her eyes. I went back to humming the tune.

The bus driver hit the lever to open the doors and lower the platform in order to load the man and his motorized scooter onto the bus. The minute the doors to the bus were opened it felt like a door to a furnace was opened, too. The inferno of heat entered our once-air-conditioned space as the man was being raised so he could enter the bus. I was thinking to myself, "If you had cut the time too short for your airport departure, right about now you might not be feeling so *happy*."

The song was into its second loop when the man wheeled onto the bus and drove the scooter to the location across from us to have its wheels locked in place for transport. I could hear a fellow male passenger huffing and puffing impatiently behind us.

The bus driver by now was sweating profusely from the heat and anxiety. I could sense his panic as he realized he was now about six minutes behind schedule. The driver moaned and grunted as sweat dripped from his forehead and he tried to move the very heavyset man on his motorized scooter backward, then forward, then backward again in an attempt to line up the wheels within the brackets on the wall to lock the wheels in position. I turned to my daughter and mouthed a very exaggerated, "Don't worry. *Beeeeee happy.*"

She wasn't happy. And as I looked around me, not many of the other people were, either. But I *was* happy. With a little help from Bobby McFerrin, I was staying very happy indeed.

The driver wiped his sweaty hands on his pants as he tried one last time to maneuver the scooter using the controls on the handlebars. This maneuvering went on for approximately three minutes when, for the first time, the man on the scooter spoke up.

He said simply, "Do you want me to get up? Would that make it easier?"

Just then, Bobby McFerrin sang, "When you worry you make it double."

I leaned over to my daughter, shrugged my shoulders, and said, "You can't make this stuff up!" I then rejoined the looping song by tapping my foot and mouthing, "Don't worry. Be happy."

I am happy to report that all the passengers on the bus that day not only made it to the airport, but also received one more Universal Lesson, whether or not they realized it at the time. Remaining in a state of joy can help us find our way to the truth, which can assist us in finding simple and obvious solutions early on instead of going to a place of fear, drama, or impatience. And learning how to stay in a state of joy and happiness during what could be a stressful situation allows us to become part of a great story that can be retold to help others enjoy life, too!

SIMPLE HUMAN TRUTH

Don't worry. Be happy.

Radiate a Joy-Filled Presence

How do people feel in your presence? We all know people who can walk into a room and light it up with their sunny personality alone. We also know others who can bring in a dark cloud behind them and change the energy from positive to negative on a moment's notice.

Decide today to be the person entering with sunshine on your shoulders. When our joy is shared, miracles become daily real-life events instead of stale passages written in books with pages yellowed by time. Mother Teresa said something wonderfully simple years ago: "Joy is a net in which you can catch souls." People want to be around joyful people. It makes them feel good, and it stirs a desire within their hearts to live the same way. Joy is the element that allows us to skip along on the path of our life rather than dragging our feet as if it is some kind of arduous journey.

Positive people with the light of joy shining from within are people that:

- Smile first
- Greet everyone, not a select few
- Cast no judgment on themselves or others
- Give sincere praise and compliments
- Lend a hand unconditionally
- Hold others up in a positive light with positive opinions, thoughts, and actions
- Speak no ill of another, in or out of that person's presence
- Live life with integrity as their base

SIMPLE HUMAN TRUTH

Joy is the element that allows us to skip along on the path of our life rather than dragging our feet as if it is some kind of arduous journey.

Build Your Joy by Decreasing Your Spending

Staying joyful is easier when we keep stress and drama out of our everyday lives. For example, shopping can be fun, but the drama created from overspending is a joy destroyer. Have you purchased a new car with large payments or a house that you cannot comfortably afford? Do you have too many credit cards? Do you secretly hide your spending from others? Many times when we add complexity to any situation joy is the first thing eliminated. Simplifying our finances is one of the ways we can simplify our lives.

Before making large purchases, we can find our way to the truth quickly by asking ourselves two questions:

Do I really need this?

Will buying this allow me to stay joyful past the excitement of the initial purchase?

As we all know, worrying about bills takes the joy away from the purchase. Keep joy in by keeping over-spending out.

Joy to Your World, A Clean Environment

Eliminating extraneous clutter in our personal environment allows us to eliminate unnecessary pollution in our minds. Have you ever heard people who say, the minute the guests arrive, "Please, excuse this mess. I've had it on my mind to clean it up, but haven't gotten around to it yet?"

Having a clean home, a clean office space, and a clean car keeps us in a joyful state, whereas disorganization in the physical world creates disarray in our mind. Dirt and clutter in these areas weigh us down and contribute to *mind pollution*. Mind pollution is created by complexity without defined direction. Adding details to our lives with material things or "things to do" is fine as long as they are manageable. The moment we begin to lose control, we add litter to our minds in the form of worry or fear, and this takes us away from the beauty we were once afforded when we kept things simple, affordable, and manageable. A well-organized world leads to a quieter mind and a more joyful existence.

On a regular basis, make sure to:

- Clean out your car each night of cups, papers, food, and so on, so it's nice and clean for your morning commute.
- Clear your home of unnecessary items that have not been used in years and sell or donate them to someone who could use them.
- Clear off your desk at the office so you have a nice, clean, uncluttered workspace that encourages efficient thinking.
- Lighten up: Dust, raise your shades, vacuum, and spring clean, even if it's winter.

A Joyful Thank You, Gratitude

Living with gratitude in your heart is one of the easiest ways to get on a joyful path that will lead you to experience all the spiritual blessings the Universe has to offer. I learned that starting each day with gratitude has had a major impact on my outlook on life and my desire to help others unconditionally. Here are some ways to travel joyfully throughout your days:

START THE DAY WITH GRATITUDE

When your eyes first blink open in the morning, say, "God, Thank you, thank you, thank you for this day." You can say it a hundred times if you feel you need to in order to feel the gratitude welling up in your heart. Don't stop until you feel the welling!

FOCUSED AND INTENTIONAL GRATITUDE

Specifying the things for which you are grateful keeps you centered in love for all things you hold dear.

You can create a positive intentional mantra, such as:

Thank you for my family, my life, my house, my job, my health, and this day. I am a grateful soul. I can see this day, this week, this month, and this year spread out before me, and they are incredible!

Staying in the present alignment of feeling "energetically" good is vital for allowing the flow of all things wonderful and spiritual into your life and for maintaining your *core power*. Core power is your internal "positive energy source." It's your personal battery that keeps you positively charged in a state of joy. Gratitude can help you do this. If you notice your energy has shifted from good to bad, you can switch it back immediately by saying, "Thank you" until you feel the shift. It really works!

Simple gratitude shifting mantra:

Thank you, thank you, thank you, thank you, thank you, thank you, thank you, thank you, thank you, thank you, thank you, thank you, thank you, thank you!

THE ATTITUDE OF GRATITUDE

Make gratitude a part of your daily life using reminders:

- Buy gratitude stones to place around your home and in your purse, briefcase, or pocket. Each time you come across the stone, take a moment to acknowledge gratitude.
- Spread gratitude around by giving the stones as gifts.
- Print out inspirational quotes about gratitude and put a new one on the mirror each week to memorize. Memorizing gratitude quotes is a conscious way to imprint words of gracious wisdom.
- Show your appreciation for others by acknowledging and expressing gratitude for the big and small things they do for you throughout your day.
- When you feel down, snap your fingers so you consciously "snap" yourself out of the doldrums. Let those bad thoughts leave your mind and allow yourself to switch back to a good thought.

SIMPLE HUMAN TRUTH

*Remaining in a state of truthful alignment ensures peace
and joy will become your faithful companions.*

* * *

Life is all about relationships with family, friends, and those in our community. As we travel throughout our days and consistently work on staying in a state of peaceful and joyful alignment, we remain centered in our hearts and not our heads. From this space of the heart we become the creators of our own stories and enjoyable events. This next chapter will show you the wonderful ways you will touch the lives of others when you infuse love into all that you do.

Love

LIVING FROM OUR HEARTS

The mind can choose to see this image in different ways.
The first way feels a bit disproportionate: the flowers almost
as tall as a mature tree. Alter your perception just a bit, how-
ever, and you will see the image three-dimensionally, with
the flowers in the foreground, the sun coming over the hori-
zon in the background, and the tree off in the distance. There
is a third way to see it, as just the word love, written 1960s
hippie-graffiti style, which is why my Guides wanted me to
paint it disproportionately.

Living from Our Hearts

When two or more hearts unite, anything is possible.

Connected Family Union

Peter and Molly's blended union of joyful souls (from left):
Mallory, Hailey, Maddy, Will, and Jake

In January 2011, my husband Peter and I were married in a beautiful and simple ceremony at a historic church in Golden Valley, Minnesota with eighty of our closest friends and family members present. My daughter Mallory and Peter's daughter Maddy were bridesmaids. Peter's sons Will and Jake were groomsmen. And my granddaughter Hailey was the flower girl.

After Peter and I exchanged vows, we had the children join us for the lighting of the Unity candle, which symbolized that we were now a connected family union. There would be no child left outside our circle of love. We wanted all souls to know that from that day forward, these children were no longer "mine" or "his." They were now and forever "ours."

Divine Union and Divine Relationship

Molly's heart rock to ground her life in love, found on a dirt path in Wisconsin in 2011

Love and truth are intimately connected. You cannot have pure love without pure truth and you cannot have pure truth without pure love. When two or more souls consciously intend to create a union with these elements in place they create a Divine Union or Divine Relationship. Connecting at the heart level allows my husband Peter and me to create a Divine Union or Divine Marriage. Connecting at the heart level with our children allows us to create Divine Relationships. Creating this soul-love connection within our family unit allows us to embrace, practice, and demonstrate Divine Union and Divine Relationships in our home.

All souls walking this earth can form a Divine Relationship when pure love and pure truth are present. In order to initiate this Divine Mission, put out the intention to ground your life in love and truth. Find a symbol that will help you to remember that love and truth are interwoven.

For example, around the time Peter and I were married, I put out the intention that I wanted to ground my life in absolute love and truth on every level. As a wedding present, a group of our neighborhood friends gave us a gift certificate for a mini-honeymoon weekend getaway at a beautiful lakeside resort in Wisconsin. The day of our arrival at the resort, my husband and I immediately donned our tennis shoes and headed off to explore the enchanting grounds. We had been walking together along a dirt path in the woods for only a short time when I tripped over the lip of a rock in the path. I looked down to see a perfect, heart-shaped rock embedded in the ground. I knew at that instant that it was meant to be my grounding rock, symbolizing the intention I had put out to the Universe. It took quite a bit of digging, but I extracted it from the path, washed it off, and brought it back to our home.

Here are some tips to ground your life in love:

- Form a Divine Partnership with your Angels and Guides. Call on them to help you manifest the perfect heart-shaped rocks, and then be on the lookout for them! You will be amazed at all the perfect, synchronistically placed heart-shaped rocks you will find as soon as you ask for assistance from the heavens.

- Once you find heart rocks that have special meaning to you, plant them around your home, office, or car. Any thing you do that is grounded in the intention of pure love and truth will produce strong roots for steady growth and a stable life journey.

- Purchase stones imprinted with the words *love* or *truth* and give them away as gifts. This gesture gives you the opportunity to tell others about your love and truth project.

SIMPLE HUMAN TRUTH

Love and truth are intimately connected.
You cannot have pure love without pure truth and
you cannot have pure truth without pure love.

Food for the Heart and Soul at the Office

A Divine Union can be unveiled in the community in many different unique and "fun-damental" ways. Call me old fashioned. I know the days of making a bag lunch and bringing it to the office have passed in favor of eating out of vending machines or foraging for food at the local fast-food franchise named after an underground transit system. But I adore my husband Peter and I want to make sure he is aware of this truth each and every day. One of the ways I show him that I love him is by packing his lunch. To be completely honest, this also gives me the opportunity to demonstrate and model consistent kindness and generosity for anyone else who might be watching as the love of my life unpacks the five plastic containers of food I have deemed his lunch for the day.

And just for kicks, every couple of weeks I'll slip a love note inside Peter's lunch bag. It makes my heart sing when he comes home later and tells me one of the guys has said, "Ooooh, what did she write on your note today?" He need not say one thing more, for I know my bag of "soul food" has worked its miracles on my husband's heart and the hearts of his coworkers once again.

SIMPLE HUMAN TRUTH
*If the way to a man's heart is initially through his stomach,
once he finds his heart, he won't need food in order to
return to this benevolent location.*

Magnify Love for Your Significant Other

Molly and the love of her life, Peter Friedenfeld

Consistently showing unconditional love and kindness for the one we call our life partner, in or out of that person's presence, is another element of Divine Union. For example, one day I was speaking on the phone with my friend Connie about future projects on which we were working. When we finished talking business, she said, "I have to tell you, I ran into your husband the other day. He is such a nice guy. You know, I've never met a man who talks so nicely about his wife as he did of you. He absolutely adores you. It was so refreshing."

When I heard Peter's kind words spoken through someone

else's lips, it magnified their power and sent a wave of love right to my heart. I've always believed one of the nicest things you can do is to speak kind words about someone behind his or her back. Peter's simple act proved this insight to be true. Later that day, I sent my husband an e-mail telling him how much it meant to me to have him say those nice things out of my presence. Connecting with him like this—at the soul-love level—feels to me like a nice warm bath with lavender salts. It's that good.

Try these simple acts of kindness that create a loving impact:

- Demonstrate love by speaking kind words out of a person's presence. The words act like magic, motivating another to do the same in return.

- Give your spouse or significant other an honest compliment on how nice he or she looks when walking by and heading out the door. A simple compliment lets your loved ones know you notice them and that they haven't become invisible to you.

- Hold your mate's hand while out in public. This gesture says; "I am consciously connected to you. I am happy to be with you. I am demonstrating our love for all to see."

- Each night before you fall asleep, hold one of your partner's hands. Take turns saying, "I love you. I love you. I love you." This simple act cements the feeling of love in your mind, body, and soul as you drift off.

SIMPLE HUMAN TRUTH

One of the nicest things you can do is to speak kind words about someone behind his or her back.

Sharing Our Lessons of Love

By integrating simple acts of kindness and love towards our partners, family members, friends, and people in the community on a daily basis, we become adept at living from our hearts. This gives us pure sight, which allows us to see clearly when another soul has traveled a great distance from the space of his or her heart.

I am a relationship person and I love people. I have always noticed—whether I was driving around looking at houses with real estate clients I'd only recently met or meeting up with good friends I hadn't seen in many years—that after we get past the initial small talk, the discussion seems to turn to children and our significant others. Another similarity I've noticed: During conversations, most souls who are *not* "en-joying" their relationships will emit the energy of silent resentment as they speak, or they will be extremely vocal about their resentment and carry an angry energy vibration with them.

For example, my former client Linda was unhappy in her relationship with her partner. She told me quite frankly that they were growing apart; the relationship had become more like a distant friendship, with each of them having a separate life, interests, hobbies, and friends. She ended her story with a simple statement: "Molly, each one of us has really stopped caring for the other."

Whenever I am afforded the opportunity to be present for another, I take it. I grab the torch of illumination and run with it, oftentimes by shining that light on my own past by saying, "I've been in your shoes, and I learned from my mistakes. Here's my story. I hope it will help you."

In this case, I asked Linda a simple question: "Is there anything that you are telling me today about all the things your boyfriend is doing wrong, or the things that are separating you from your love for one another, that you haven't told him yourself?"

She looked at me and asked, "What do you mean?"

I repeated the question slowly to help her absorb its importance and to give her time to move from her head down to her heart.

She then answered sheepishly, "Well, no, I haven't talked to him about a lot of these things. He wouldn't listen anyway, and it's too much work."

I replied, "After my first marriage ended in divorce, one of the main things I realized was that I was fifty percent responsible for everything that went right, and fifty percent responsible for everything that went wrong in that relationship. There were many times I should have stayed current but didn't. By 'being current' I mean not allowing disagreements or hurtful behavior to be deposited into my past without having a conversation or making a loving correction to return us both to the space of our hearts. Many times, I was responsible for stuffing words, thoughts, and conversations away without resolution. He and I grew resentful of each other about issues unspoken. As a result, we grew apart. I know now that if there is something that doesn't feel right in any relationship, it's my responsibility as well as the other person's to be sure to stay current on topics and conversations." I went on, "I need to 'out' anything that feels like we've veered off track, gotten out of alignment, right then and there, with love."

Linda took my advice, and it made me feel great that I was able to guide her through a difficult time.

Simple Wisdom

Think back to a time in your life when you may have experienced severe pain, trauma, sorrow, or anger because of something you did or that someone did to you. What was the one thing that finally snapped you out of feeling bad? The shift out of feeling bad most likely arrived on the heels of love. Perhaps what lifted your spirits were the feelings of love that flowed from the heart of another, embodied in their kind words or actions right when you needed them most.

The day I met with Linda, she was very unhappy in her relationship with her boyfriend. The story of simple wisdom shared from my personal life experience, delivered with compassion and humility, landed on her heart. My story helped her to see things from her boyfriend's point of view, and I believe it also helped her to understand that she shared half the responsibility for bringing joy back into her relationship with him. Looking at the situation in this new light allowed Linda to visualize herself and her boyfriend as a team rather than opponents out to catch the other doing something wrong.

Our personal stories of perseverance contain immense wisdom that can assist others in finding their way to peace and illumination during difficult times. This kind of loving helps us to realize that all of us are, collectively, a team. If we work together with love as the foundation in all our relationships, we can take any situation that contains a hardship and turn it into a teaching opportunity.

SIMPLE HUMAN TRUTH

Our personal stories of perseverance contain immense wisdom that can assist others in finding their way to peace and illumination during difficult times.

Keeping Relationships in Alignment

As Linda learned, holding ourselves and other souls accountable for inappropriate or unloving actions or comments as they occur is vital to keeping relationships in alignment. Once we allow something inappropriate or unloving to go unchecked and without resolution, it is as if we have taken out our spiritual suitcase and stuffed this new item of unresolved pain or anger into it. We may not see it, but we carry it with us, with the result that over time we begin to feel weighed down with resentment from all the unresolved emotions generated by things that bother us about other people.

We begin to try to catch them doing something wrong instead of seeing all the things they are doing right. We fill in the blanks of mental conversations never spoken aloud, and *assume* that the other person should know what we are thinking and feeling without our initiating the necessary communication to keep the love flowing and the relationship in alignment. This behavior results in a spiraling pattern of negativity instead of a blossoming pattern of positive, loving growth. We then lose interest in working on keeping the relationship fresh and vibrant, and it soon becomes stale and lifeless.

SIMPLE HUMAN TRUTH
Love is the ultimate creator.

The Peacemaker

Unconditional love, kindness, forgiveness, and patience are key in the process of working together to break conditional love patterns that do not serve our souls. This wisdom is transferrable to any relationship between two or more people, including co-workers, friends, relatives, and neighbors.

If you have discord in your home, school, or workplace, face each situation in a state of PEACE, LOVE, and TRUTH and stay current throughout the reconciliation process.

A Peacemaker says:

- Tomorrow is a new and glorious day and whatever went wrong today will be different in twenty-four hours.
- I am the creator of how my life will play out and I choose to live "drama free" and to enjoy this journey.
- I don't have to prove I'm right. The truth is always revealed with perfect Divine Timing and lessons are dispensed in Divine Order and with Divine Reason.
- I am a Peacemaker and everyone is responsible for growing his or her own soul. I can assist when asked, but will not demand understanding from another.

SIMPLE HUMAN TRUTH
If you have discord in your home, school or workplace, face each situation within a state of PEACE, LOVE, and TRUTH and stay current throughout the reconciliation process.

Breaking the Cruelty Pattern with Love

Our hearts respond best to kindness. Becoming a Peacemaker assists us in avoiding negative patterns that can inflict pain on another. One of these patterns is pushing people's buttons with the intention of firing them up in a negative way, creating drama on a moment's notice. One of the many ways we do this is with cruelty. Cruel words are *energy knives* or *energy arrows* thrown or shot at another's heart. Our hearts do respond to cruelty ... by building walls or shutting down.

We are spirits in a human body. When we say "mean spirited" things, we are in fact being *mean spirits*. The person dispensing cruel words has a single intention, to inflict pain. Cruelty contains no love in its delivery, so no message of love is received at the heart level. Instead, when messages are delivered with cruelty, judgment, deceit, or anger, the information is immediately sent to the recipient's brain for processing.

The ego takes over as a form of protection, and he or she usually reacts by "shooting from the hip," sending something negative in return.

We all know that if we throw a ball at a wall, it will bounce right back at us. This is what occurs when we meet negativity with negativity. If we want to grow, the way to break a pattern of negativity is to face anything negative with love.

SIMPLE HUMAN TRUTH
If we want to grow, the way to break a pattern of negativity is to face anything negative with love.

Joking with Knives

Another way we dispense cruelty and create distance with words is by what I call *joking with knives*. We aim demeaning comments at another soul, disguised as a harmless jab or a joke. We know when we are on the receiving end of joking with knives because the remarks are cutting in nature and the only person not laughing is us.

It is our job to hold ourselves and all souls walking this planet accountable for unloving behavior. When we do this by staying current, responding lovingly as a situation occurs, we promote soul growth that builds the foundation of positive change to assist all humanity. Kind actions toward another leave a positive imprint on the heart. Cruel words cut like knives and create battle scars. Leave a wake of kindness, not a wake of destruction, wherever you go.

By teaching others how to treat us using kind words and kind behavior, we build our core strength and core integrity. This process allows us to become aligned with our heart. Once we are in alignment with our heart, we know accepting unacceptable behavior does not show love to ourselves or to the other person.

SIMPLE HUMAN TRUTH
Kind actions towards another leave a positive imprint on the heart.

Kind, Corrective Words

Some of the cruelest people you may ever know have never been shown an ounce of kindness in their lifetime or experienced the powerful changes that can occur with kind, corrective words. All it takes is someone to be the first to face negativity with love and thus begin the process of weakening the grip of deep-rooted patterns. Speaking kind words starts a wave of love in motion that brings more love upon your shores.

The moment cruel words are spoken, state your truth kindly, right then and there. Loving adjustments made at the time of occurrence bring souls back into the alignment of love. A vital component of breaking any pattern of cruelty is not allowing inappropriate behavior to go unchecked without the injection of a loving correction.

These examples of speaking the truth apply for most instances of cruelty:

"Those words are not kind and loving."

"That doesn't feel right."

"That hurts my heart."

"That behavior undermines our relationship."

SIMPLE HUMAN TRUTH

Speaking kind words starts a wave of love in motion that brings more love upon your shores.

Traveling to a Positive Place

There is great power in our words, because they are thoughts to which we have given additional energy by speaking them aloud so another person can know them. Travel only to a positive place with your thoughts, words, and actions—for yourself and for others—and you will begin to notice immediate results as the positive shifting occurs.

Our unspoken thoughts are also powerful. If we can get really good at recognizing when a negative thought pops in, deleting it, and canceling it out by immediately replacing it with a positive thought, then we begin to change for the better and more easily remain in a joyful vibration location. By training our minds to travel only to positive places, we can make positive changes in our relationships and our lives.

SIMPLE HUMAN TRUTH
There is great power in our words, because they are thoughts to which we have given additional energy by speaking them aloud so another person can know them.

Holding Yourself and Others Up in the Light of Love

Do you know people that say negative things? Comments like…
"He'll never amount to anything."
"I can't stand how I look."

THE BOOK OF SIMPLE HUMAN TRUTHS

"She is so self centered."

"He's a space cadet."

"I can't do anything right."

"My teenager has no personal motivation."

"My ex-wife or ex-husband is such a horrible parent."

When we speak in this way, we are creating an almost prayerful intention for ourselves or the other person to stay in the location we have placed them with our negative words. If we say, "My good-for-nothing ex-husband is such a horrible parent," isn't that what we are hoping for? For our ex-husband to remain, "good for nothing"? That sentence certainly isn't intended to encourage the ex-husband to make changes for the better. And lest we forget, we chose this soul to help us produce another soul. We made the choice for him to become the parent of our child in the first place.

Our words manifest in our personal lives. Switch anything negative to the positive by envisioning the person changing for the better, with the ultimate goal of standing in—and seeing them in—a positive light.

To visualize all in a positive, loving light:

- Picture yourself or another person in your mind's eye.
- Place a bubble of clear energy around yourself or the other person.
- Fill the bubble with beautiful white light sent down from the heavens.
- Repeat the process, sending down pink love light from the heavens to fill the bubble.
- Visualize yourself or the other person in this light of love. See the heart softening and growing. Imagine yourself or the other person making positive decisions, changes for the better, and crossing the finish line with arms raised above the head in victory!

- Complete the visualization by sending love from your pure heart to the soul in the bubble of light. Even if it's your own!

Note: You can send love to multiple people at one time during a single visualization if you wish. For example: Place your entire family in a bubble of love and light and send them all pure love.

Fairygiveness

Hailey, the "magic magnet" at four years old, exhibiting her Fairy-like joy to the world

Forgiveness is vital in the soul-growth process. Just as you and I have made numerous missteps or mistakes, so have those we love most. Forgiving another does not condone a violation against you. Rather, forgiveness exists for you to release the pain from the event so you can move forward. Leave the life lesson that the other soul must learn in the hands of the Universe. For each action there is a reaction and the Universe is well aware of this fact. Placing faith in Divine Order and Divine Reason allows us to say with confidence, "I forgive so I can live."

Our seven-year-old granddaughter understands this Universal Truth, which constantly amazes and delights me. Hailey loves to sleep over at our house whenever she can, and my husband Peter and I love spending time with her. One night I had just given Hailey a nice warm bath and was getting her ready for bed when she said, "Grandma, I know why I'm here."

I said, "You do? Tell me, why are you here?"

She answered with the commanding wisdom of a person wise beyond her years. "I'm here to love everyone and help people forgive each other…Forgiveness is easy with Angels, Grandma. I call it *fairygiveness*."

My heart stopped and time did, too. Have you ever experienced love so profound that the illusion of time became lengthened, allowing you to savor the moment past the normal physical bounds so you could enjoy it for just one, two, or three seconds more? That is what happened that day with Hailey as we stood next to a tub full of bathwater.

"What a teacher," I thought as I combed her hair and took a picture in my mind of her Angelic face. I wanted to let that specific time fragment dissolve into every cell of my body so my spirit would never, ever forget its simple message. I wanted to cement my feelings of unconditional love for this child of the Angelic Kingdom who is currently walking this earth.

"She speaks the truth," I said in my head, and felt that truth so strongly that I repeated, "This little Angel speaks the truth."

(Many of our young people are, in fact, very wise souls, placed here to facilitate the return of love and truth. You can spot one of these children, beautiful beings mature beyond their years, a mile away because they are the ones teaching us adults some pretty incredible life lessons. In spiritual circles these children are called the Indigo and Crystal Children. Many of them will speak to you about Fairies and Angels and maintain close connections with relatives who have already made the transition to the light. These wonderful souls already know their life purpose. All you have to do is ask them, and you will be amazed at the answers if you stop long enough to listen to their stories. If you have an Indigo or Crystal Child in your life, talk about the things she brings up in conversation. Let her speak her truth and love her unconditionally as she reveals her world to you.)

Forgiveness Is the Key that Unlocks Learning and Spiritual Growth

Forgiveness (fairygiveness) is easy, as Hailey says. All we have to do is to remember to forgive, and never forget that as we travel along our paths we have made mistakes that have hurt others too. Some of our mistakes may have been minor; others may have resulted in tragedy or inflicted incredible pain upon another. If we take a moment to reflect on the memory of a time we may have hurt another and can re-experience the gratitude we felt when we realized we were forgiven, this helps us to understand the power of forgiveness. Conversely, we may be able to think of one or many people in our current lives whom we may not have granted forgiveness, or who have not forgiven us. Many of us desire or demand that forgiveness be granted us easily and quickly, yet we do not grant forgiveness to another in return. This simple reflection exercise allows us to see and feel the negative impact an unforgiving heart has on life's precious relationships.

Wounds that don't heal are the result of our mentally traveling back in time with an unforgiving heart to pick at sores by reliving the violation or tragedy over and over. Give the gift of forgiveness to another. The blessings you will receive will be an immediate flowing of love and a sense of release. This process helps you return to a joyful state of being, release negative energy from the event, and move forward in learning.

SIMPLE HUMAN TRUTH

If someone is facing a difficult time, one of the kindest things you can do for him or her is to say, "I'm just going to love you through this."

Bringing It Back Around, the Angelic Way

This next story shows the ease and grace of forgiveness when you call in the Angels for assistance. Back in December 2011, a woman dropped into our Violet Wisdom Inspiration Radio show chat room during a discussion of how heavenly Angels can help us with reconciliation and forgiveness. She said that she had put out the prayerful intention to forgive and asked her personal Angels to bring back around all the people in her life with whom she needed to reconcile. In so doing, she hoped to learn to be more loving and resolve any unfinished business that was preventing her soul from moving forward in growth in the area of forgiveness. The woman said the entire process took a couple of years, but her Angels did bring every person back around. She forgave herself, granted forgiveness, asked for forgiveness, and spoke her truth.

Heart-centered forgiveness ensures purity in its release. Purity prevents negative fragments of any kind from being left behind without resolution. Instead, the slate is clean and the heart expands to release the pain or sorrow attached to the initial event, incident, or violation. Fairygiveness is simple and clean. It allows forgiveness to flow into our lives straight through our hearts.

SIMPLE HUMAN TRUTH
Heart-centered forgiveness ensures purity in its release.

Delivering Your Message with Love

Have you ever tried to sneeze with your eyes open? I'm not even sure it's possible without your eyeballs popping out of your head from the pressure, so I've never tried it. But I'm pretty sure it would not end well. Delivering an important message without being centered in your heart will most likely not end well either. Once dispensed, your intended message may sound shallow, with little emotion behind it. It may be heard by the other party, but most likely will land flat and as a result will not be received into the recipient's heart.

In order for your message to be received, the recipient needs to be able to feel the love and truth contained within the words on a soul level. This result is achieved when the message we dispense originates from our hearts. Grounding our message in love and truth tells our souls, and the other person, that we intend to keep our ego out of it.

How to deliver messages with love, truth, and kindness:

- Hold your hand over your heart to center yourself in your heart space and feel the love welling up inside you.
- Check your message content for purity. The content of the message should be love-based and truth-based, delivered with kindness and without judgment, preaching, ego, or any intent to control the outcome.
- Prepare the message by eliminating words like *should, must, need,* or *have to*—these are immediate red flags that we are trying to control a person's growth by telling someone what to do. Every person has free will to make the right or wrong choice. How your heartfelt message is *received* is not in your control. You only have control over how your message is delivered.
- Deliver the message according to the Golden Rule (*Treat others as you would like to be treated*). In your mind, turn the situation around and imagine that you are on the receiving end of the message you are about to deliver. If it does not feel right, change the delivery or revise the message until you feel that if the same message were delivered to you, it would be received right into your heart and soul.
- Keep your message simple and to the point.

Coming Home

The process of connecting and loving from our hearts feels wonderful and natural. We find ourselves hugging people more. We truly appreciate people more. And most importantly, we don't want anyone to leave our presence without feeling loved. This heart connection, when locked in place, feels like coming home after a long trip: comfortable, warm, and grounding.

Signs you are living from your heart include:

- Speaking with your hand over your heart
- Finding that *love* becomes the new four-letter word in your vocabulary
- Being drawn to heart-shaped objects
- Cherishing quotes about love, love-themed music, and loved-based movies
- More deeply appreciating inspirational stories, or finding yourself telling or creating stories of your own
- Investing as much interest in other people as in yourself
- Feeling compelled to perform more compassion-based Spiritual Samaritan acts on behalf of others, unconditionally
- Hugging people more often and displaying affection freely and easily
- Consciously checking your behavior and speech to make sure you stay in a Divine Relationship with people
- Arriving at the knowledge that judging others prevents you from being a compassionate soul
- Becoming more forgiving and caring

SIMPLE HUMAN TRUTH
It is all for naught, if not for love.

Sending Love on the Go

Sending love to others, anywhere and at any time, is very easy. You can send love while you are walking, waiting for a plane, or even standing in line at the grocery store. (It doesn't matter if you do it aloud or in your head; the effect is the same.)

Here's how:

- Think of all the people in your life that you love.
- Begin by stating the name of one person at a time. (For example: John Doe.) "John Doe, I love you. I love you. I love you."
- Go on to the next person. "Jane Smith, I love you. I love you. I love you."
- Repeat the steps until you mention all the people you love.
- Once you've gone through the list of all the people you love on this physical plane, you may continue by sending love to all the souls that have passed on before you.
- Next, send love by naming the people with whom you are currently having a difficult time or you need to forgive in some way.
- Last, state from your heart, "Let peace and love reign in my world."

SIMPLE HUMAN TRUTH

If we could all love each and every person that crosses our path a little bit more, we could attain inner peace with the knowledge that many people on this planet would be hurting a whole lot less.

***

There is no heart that beats in a human being or earthly creature that does not respond positively to love and kindness. It is simple kindness that paves the way for love to flow in freely and land upon a weary heart. The next chapter will explain why this is so.

KINDNESS IS EVERLASTING

In this image, a soul is walking on the earth. Its whole life leaves a trail: its gift to earth and its fellow humans. Its life creates the earth. It is the earth. Like a ball of twine, the soul's dreams and creations are strung together, moment by moment, from everything it puts forth from its being. Not always sure of what will become of what it gives or leaves behind, the soul steps forward with love and intends beauty, trusting that the Wisdom of the One will collaborate with it and enable the unfolding of optimal beauty and light, bringing joy to all.

Kindness Is Everlasting

Words of love cast from thy lips
reach another heart at lightning speed.

Compassion Lesson at the Shopping Mall

My first lesson in extending kindness on a moment's notice appeared when I was nineteen years old. It was the first serious, adult lesson I can remember acknowledging, but I guarantee that thousands upon thousands of such lessons had already been presented to me before this turning point.

It was 1984. I had moved out to Los Angeles on a whim because I wanted to escape the snowy Minnesota winters and the well-meaning guidance of my parental units, thank you very much! I loved the pulse of the sprawling city, the sunshine, and the energy there, and I soon felt at home.

One day when I was entering the Glendale Galleria shopping mall, I learned the truth of the adage, "When one door closes, another one opens." For my spiritual door began to open after I shut the door on two elderly ladies. I was in a hurry that day as I blasted by the women with the speed of a gazelle. My judgmental ego registered these women as old and slow. That thought was followed by self-praise as I patted myself on the back for being so young and agile.

My spiritually immature brain didn't recognize that immense wisdom is everywhere. It's flying by us at lightning speed, and it's up to us to decide whether we are going to grab a net and catch some as it heads on by. Once at the door, I hurriedly flung it open and proceeded inside without holding it for the two ladies. As the door began to shut, I heard one of them say, "My, that young girl was rude." I rolled my eyes in utter annoyance and kept going.

I kept going and going and going for another four years without the slightest thought of that encounter until, at twenty-three years old, I became a mother and grew more mature and less selfish. Motherhood will change you. It allows you to take the focus off yourself and place your attention and unconditional love on another human.

It was now my turn to enter a shopping mall, this time without so much forward movement as I enjoyed four years earlier. I had a stroller, a diaper bag, a baby, but only two arms, and was faced with doors that needed to be opened manually. I then realized how wonderful and refreshing it is when someone else offers the gift of loving kindness by simply holding a door open for a few seconds so another human can move forward freely.

At that precise moment, my selfish encounter with the two elderly ladies came flooding back into my mind, complete with the words, "My, that young girl was rude."

And thus arrived my boomerang lesson from the Universe to show me what it's like to be on the other side of the door, so to speak. My lesson was simple. Never be too much in a hurry to help a fellow human and always keep humility in check, for some day you may need the assistance of another. This time I got the message.

When you receive a boomerang lesson or other message of wisdom from the Universe, acknowledge it and begin utilizing it to demonstrate and reinforce your learning, cement it in place, and show gratitude for the lesson. For example, ever since I received, acknowledged and absorbed my message, I have been very conscientious about holding the door open for my fellow human. I may never be able to thank those elderly ladies in person for helping me learn one of life's big lessons, but I've thanked them many times over in spirit.

SIMPLE HUMAN TRUTH

When you receive your message of wisdom from the Universe, acknowledge it and begin utilizing it to demonstrate and reinforce your learning, cement it in place, and show gratitude for the lesson.

The Love-and-Kindness Caffeine Experiment

Just as in the story above, you may be asked to extend spontaneous kindness to another soul you will never see again or, as this next story shows, to extend your kind energy to another you see on a daily basis.

Back when I worked in an office, I use to joke that our coffee machine water line must have been hooked up to the Minneapolis toilet water system. Seriously, the coffee it produced tasted that bad. So each morning, instead of drinking coffee made with toilet water, my friends Gary, Barb, and I would visit the coffee shop across the street. Upon our arrival, without fail, the young woman at the counter would ask us tersely, "What do you want?" And each day I would place the same order, a small black coffee with room for cream. The ritual became like a scene from the movie

Groundhog Day: The same terse greeting, met with my ordering the same cup of coffee. We were into the second week of placing our identical coffee orders and receiving the identical response when an idea popped into my head. I told my friends, "I am going to perform a love-and-kindness caffeine experiment." They laughed, as they had no idea what I was talking about.

I elaborated. "A love-and-kindness caffeine experiment is something I am creating right now. I'm going to shower this woman with genuine love and kindness and see if that makes a difference in her demeanor." I continued, "I have a feeling she has seldom seen either of these things demonstrated in her life." So each morning, off we went to the coffee shop. But now, in addition to placing my coffee-*Groundhog-Day* order, I would say with sincerity something nice.

The first day of my experiment, I told the girl, "I don't even know your name. My name is Molly, and these are my friends Barb and Gary. What's your name?"

"My name is April," she answered without looking up.

I replied truthfully, "I really like that name. It's very nice."

The second day, we went in and I said, "Hi, April. I'm Molly. Remember me? I'll take a small coffee with room for cream. Thank you."

The third day, I greeted April as usual, but this time she replied, "I know, small coffee with room for cream."

That simple statement made me smile, because it showed my friends and me how quickly this love-and-kindness caffeine experiment was producing results.

By the end of that first week, April now greeted us as we came in the door: "Hey, Molly, I'll get your black coffee with room for cream."

I replied sincerely, "Thanks, April, for remembering my order."

The love-and-kindness caffeine experiment taught each one

of us that love and kindness, like cream and sugar, are ingredients that can turn a bland encounter in to an inspirational story demanding to be retold. When we take the time to crack open someone's door with heartfelt kindness, the light of love is then granted access, shining through to reach the recipient's heart. This process creates a positive shift and change at the soul level. Love and kindness are the hammer and chisel that gently chip through barriers and long-held beliefs to reveal the magnificent soul contained within every human.

SIMPLE HUMAN TRUTH

Love and kindness are the hammer and chisel that gently chip through barriers and long-held beliefs to reveal the magnificent soul contained within every human.

Spreading Love and Kindness Far and Wide

In a love-and-kindness experiment, love is the foundation on which your encounter is built, and showing kindness should be your only motive. A clear indicator that your experiment is successful is when you feel the love welling inside your own heart as you see changes occurring as a result of your efforts. Allowing love and kindness to be dispensed in this patient and caring way creates miracles in the lives of all involved.

How to spread love and kindness:

- Put out the intention to live with love and kindness as the foundation of your life and give them away freely and unconditionally, trusting that you have a limitless supply, because you do!
- Have compassion for and a vested interest in all souls, not just immediate family and friends.
- Scan your heart in each encounter with another to make sure your intentions are true, noble, and selfless. This will ensure that you never miss a beat to show love and kindness.
- Greet everyone you meet with a smile, hug, or kind word or thought.

SIMPLE HUMAN TRUTH

If you are having a bad day, take the focus off of yourself by giving someone an honest compliment using kind words, or by performing a kind act to help them along their way. Extending kindness to another allows you to become kinder to yourself, too!

Lightworkers in Radio

My days working in radio back in the 1990s created some of my most poignant memories about spreading kindness, joy, and love. My station's general manager, Rolf Pepple, had a remarkable way of motivating and guiding his employees to join him in his passion for making money and, in the process, touching the lives of others in unique and positive ways. He created a magical office environment and all of us knew how lucky they were to be able to work there.

Rolf gave up control when necessary and entrusted his employees to spearhead and implement heart-centered events around the Twin Cities. He encouraged us all to become "beacons of light" in the community and to come up with innovative ways to implement outreach programs. All ideas were valued, none discounted. Over the years, we read books to inner-city children at a school down the street from the station during our lunch breaks, passed out free pumpkins and trick-or treat-bags at Halloween and, thanks to generous donations from a local tree growers' association, we gave away hundreds of real Christmas trees complete with lights and ornaments to those in need during the holiday season.

These kind projects softened hearts, educated youth, and turned fellow employees into one big family, thereby creating a cohesive, loyal, and productive team of employees too! Compassion brings out the essence of the Lightworker. Sometimes, all it takes is one person to unite an army of Lightworkers, leading the way through volunteerism in a unified direction of love. When people join hearts collectively, our love expands and is spread out across the world like an endless wave of sunshine, changing everything in its path in ways we once thought impossible.

SIMPLE HUMAN TRUTH
Sometimes, all it takes is one person to unite an army of Lightworkers, leading the way through volunteerism in a unified direction of love.

Expanding Hearts Through Kind Thoughts, Words, and Deeds

Spreading kindness in the community when you are by yourself is simple, too! Here are some easy tips to get you started:

IN THE CAR:

- Wave someone into a long line of traffic.
- Use your blinkers so people know your intentions.
- Allow someone to have the parking lot spot you had your eye on, just because.
- If someone is cruel to you while you are driving, say a prayer of compassion and forgiveness and ask God to soften their heart and yours.
- Be respectful of driving laws.

AT THE STORE:

- Pick merchandise up off the floor if it falls off the rack.
- Place a loose grocery cart in the cart corral in the parking lot so the wind doesn't send it into another vehicle.
- If a cashier gave you too much change, politely state the error so you both can make it right.
- If the customer before you in line gave the clerk a difficult time, step up to the counter with a smile and cancel out the bad experience.

AT THE OFFICE:

- Show up on time for work each day and give your employer the full number of hours for which you are being paid.

- Lead by example. Show others your strong work ethic regardless of what anyone else is modeling around you.
- Be a networker: Coordinate a specific lunchtime to join with others and build a sense of community at work.
- Spread kind words to all those around you—compliment good behavior, recognize accomplishments, and show gratitude when you see someone doing something right.

AT SCHOOL:

- Model accountability, attendance, and punctuality.
- Teach your child about respecting authority and rules.
- Teach your child how to show love, kindness, and compassion to fellow students and teachers.
- Hold your child accountable for cruel behavior, words, or actions directed toward another.
- Look your children in the eye and listen to them with interest when inquiring about their day.

Gracious Receiving

How you respond when someone is loving toward you is also important. If someone has kind words for you, graciously thank them. Accepting compliments rather than discounting them allows many wonderful things to occur:

- It allows the other person to bless you and feeds your spirit.
- It blesses the person giving the compliment with a feeling of worth by being a part of brightening your day.
- It gives you both the opportunity to pay the kindness energy forward so you can collectively spread it to others.

SIMPLE HUMAN TRUTH
Spread LOVE and KINDNESS wherever you go.
Then you can be sure you are never far from it!

Kindness Creates Lifetime Memories

This next story shows why graciously receiving a kind compliment opens up even more unique blessings. In February 2012, I met up for lunch with my co-workers Beth and Mary from the good old radio days. I hadn't seen my friend Beth, in particular, for many years. The moment she sat down, she said, "I told my daughter Alison that I was coming to see you for lunch today. She is in her first year of college now, and she wanted me to tell you hello." Beth continued, "Alison always thought you were one of the coolest adults she had ever met."

I was floored. I said, "Really? Why would she think that?"

Beth replied with a big smile on her face. "Alison remembers the times she was at the radio station with another employee's daughter. The girls loved how each time they would come to visit, you measured them up against the wall in your office to see how much they had grown since the last time you saw them. She remembers your fun personality and how you were really good at making people feel happy."

The memory of those times flooded into my mind. Now I was the one with a big smile on my face. "That's so funny," I said. "I remember that!"

I now understood how that could be such a fond memory for two eight-year-old girls. As Beth, Mary, and I sat talking, I took a moment and reflected back to one of the fondest memories from my own childhood. Each September, before we went back to school, my father lined us four siblings up with our backs to the basement door so he could mark the spot behind our heads to see how much we had grown over the summer. Even our Beagle-Basset Hound, Charlie, was included and measured in this growth ritual.

I left the lunch that day with two life lessons learned: We touch hearts with kindness in simple ways, and an act of kindness may take only a moment of our time, but when captured in the heart the memory lives forever.

SIMPLE HUMAN TRUTH

An act of kindness may take only a moment of our time,
but when captured in the heart the memory lives forever.

The Painted Turtle

Kind acts not only live forever in the heart, but also are effective teaching tools. One of the coolest things I have experienced since the birth of my granddaughter more than seven years ago is that whenever an animal or human needs assistance or a prayer, she happens to be with me. I affectionately call her my little "magic magnet," for I know there is always a great purpose behind each one of these divinely guided spiritual encounters.

Hailey and I were in the car and had just turned onto the road, leaving one of her favorite parks. We'd been traveling for less than a minute when I noticed a painted turtle up ahead, trying desperately to cross to the other side of the road as cars drove over it between their tires.

I announced, "Hailey, we have a turtle to save! Are you ready?"

Hailey said in return, "Yes, Grandma. Save him!"

I pulled safely off the road and rolled down the window so Hailey could watch a good deed in action (and give me direction if needed from her car seat). I got out and, as I stood by the side of the road, cars continued rolling over the turtle as it tried to cross. I was dumbfounded as to why people wouldn't stop or slow down for one minute so I could pick up the creature and move it.

So I did what any kindergarten crossing guard would do. I raised my hand at the next car that approached and said, "Stop!" The driver halted the moment I raised my hand. I stooped down, picked up the painted turtle, and brought him or her (I'm not sure which—I didn't pay much attention in science class) to its intended destination.

I heard Hailey yell from the window. "We saved him, Grandma!"

After I got back in the car Hailey said again, "We saved that turtle, didn't we, Grandma."

I said, "Absolutely!"

A few minutes later, we were back on the highway, heading east, when we came upon an illuminated billboard. These billboards change every twenty seconds or so, beaming a new digital advertisement. As we approached, the billboard changed, and up popped an ad for the Minnesota Zoo. The image that flashed across it was a larger-than-life photo of a painted turtle.

I shouted, "Hailey, look, that turtle is thanking us for saving its life!"

What are the chances that we would save a painted turtle and then moments later pass by a billboard that just happens to change to a picture of a painted turtle the minute we drive by it? I'm not a betting woman. I don't even like casinos, but I bet the odds are about a *ba-jillion* to one. This, my friends, is what a spiritual sign from our Angels and Spirit Guides looks like. I believe they were saying, "Thank you, ladies, for taking the time to save one of God's creatures."

People learn about kindness in many different ways. Some of us learn by demonstration and others by getting involved. However you learn is right for you; what's important is to be open to the learning process so you can grow your spirit.

Directing Traffic

We can offer kind assistance in many ways. Sometimes a soul may need assistance from a person with focused direction and a peaceful presence in order to guide them out of a difficult circumstance. That's what happened another time, on a hot summer day back in 2009, when I had just picked up my little "magic magnet" from daycare. Within moments of Hailey's appearance in my car, we spotted a young girl in her twenties who needed our help. She was frustrated, crying because her car had stalled in the middle of a busy intersection.

I said, "Hailey, that girl needs us. Will you be OK if I help her for a moment?"

Hailey immediately replied, "Yes, Grandma, go help her."

I parked the car off to the side of the road and reached the girl in the truck, who was still crying.

She said, "I told my dad this truck was going to die."

I replied, "No worries, we'll get you out of the intersection."

As cars buzzed past us without stopping, I made eye contact with a man driving by and pointed at him to pull over. I thought to myself. "I must have been a traffic cop in a past life. This directing traffic comes way too easy."

The man pulled over as instructed and we guided the beat-up

truck off the road and parked it next to my car. I thanked the man for his kind assistance and sent him on his way, and then returned to the girl, who had started crying once again.

"Now, my cell phone is dead," she fumed.

I quickly replied. "No worries, here's mine."

She made the call and connected with her father so he could come and assist her. Crisis solved.

When I returned to the car, Hailey had a smile on her face. She said, "We helped her, didn't we Grandma?"

I said, "Yes, Hailey, we sure did."

A month later, in the car once again and traveling to yet another destination, Hailey said, "Grandma, remember when *we* helped that crying girl with her truck that wouldn't work?"

These repeated statements let me know this truth: Role-modeling behavior with unconditional love and kindness as its foundation never goes unnoticed. Hailey hadn't gotten out of the car that day, but she put forth loving energy for that girl just as I did—right from her car seat!

SIMPLE HUMAN TRUTH

Role-modeling behavior with unconditional love and kindness as its foundation never goes unnoticed.

Birds of a Feather Flock Together

Earthly Angels Ethan Weiser (top) with Nikhil Pandey (bottom)
saving a baby Purple Martin in Wayzata, Minnesota

When you join together with others as a spontaneous team to accomplish kind deeds, this is when you will really have something to "tweet" about. In July 2012, Hailey was staying with my husband and me for the week while she attended an acting class. It was an exceptionally beautiful summer night. Hailey and I love to be outdoors, so we jumped in the car and headed in the direction of her favorite park. We were just blocks away when the feeling came over me to try something different.

I said, "Hailey, How about we try a new park tonight?"

Hailey replied, "Sure, Grandma."

That was all I needed to hear, and off we went in the opposite direction.

We arrived at a new park, minutes from our house in a little town called Wayzata, at around 7 p.m. As we got out of the car I immediately directed Hailey's attention to the sky. Hundreds of Purple Martins (a petite bird similar to a swallow) were gliding and swooping over our heads, catching bugs in the evening sky. To the left of the park entrance stood a large birdhouse situated atop a ten-foot pole. We approached a little girl who had a baby bird in front of her on the ground beneath the birdhouse.

"Oh, no!" Hailey exclaimed. "The baby fell out of the nest."

I asked Hailey and the little girl, "How are we going to get this baby bird back up in its nest?"

If possible, I try to involve children in Spiritual Samaritan efforts so they become part of an earthly Angel team.

Within minutes, two teenage boys walked past and an idea popped in. I scanned their height and thought to myself, "If I have this boy stand on that boy's shoulders, that would close the ten-foot gap and we could put the baby bird back up in its nest."

I approached the boys as they sat down on the swings about thirty feet away to talk and relax. Smiling, I quickly yet casually stated my purpose before they felt compelled to tell me to skedaddle out of their space, "Are you boys interested in saving a baby bird?"

One of the boys, wearing glasses, looked up with a perplexed expression on his face. I pointed and stated, "See that tall birdhouse over there? One of the baby birds fell out of its nest and we are trying to save it."

I directed my next question to the other boy. "Can you help us by standing on your friend's shoulders?"

I was amazed at how enthusiastically they both answered, "Sure we can."

The boy with the glasses went on to say, "We stand on each other's shoulders all the time in acting class."

I smiled inside. "Hmmm, I smell synchronicity all over this rescue."

The boys followed me to the birdhouse and the slightly smaller boy jumped up on his friend's shoulders while holding onto the birdhouse pole for support. His friend was shaking and quivering below, trying to keep his balance as best he could. I knew that Cirque Du Soleil would not be calling either one of these young lads for an upcoming road show, but I didn't care; they were doing earthly Angel work right here and now.

I picked up the baby bird and on my tiptoes handed him to the boy who would place the creature in its nest. Once the baby bird was safely returned to his home I said, "Strike a pose for a picture."

I snapped a photo on my phone and texted the boys the picture right on the spot so they could share the experience with their friends. When we involve others in spontaneous acts of kindness, we go from being strangers to becoming a united team connected at the heart level.

Hailey and I smiled at each other and headed over to the tire swing with love and joy in our hearts for a job well done.

(Months later, I came across the meaning of this specific bird animal totem and was in awe of the synchronistic meaning and how connected this was to our specific bird-saving operation. Here it is: Purple Martin energy teaches cooperation, establishing peace, and shows the importance of teamwork and community action.)

SIMPLE HUMAN TRUTH
When we involve others in spontaneous acts of kindness,
we go from being strangers to becoming a united team
connected at the heart level.

Sleeping Behind the Wheel

Molly with Jake at twelve years old, the age of his
"Sleeping Behind the Wheel" initiation

As my adventures with Hailey show, we can create magic in the relationships with our children in many different, *kind* ways. This next story demonstrates how to create a wonderful bond by having childlike fun. It's easy.

When I began dating my husband Peter, his son Jake had just turned twelve years old. I wanted to make sure Jake knew I loved being around him. One of my first opportunities alone with him came when he needed a ride to hockey practice one day after school.

To break the ice on the way to the rink I asked, "Have you ever heard of 'Sleeping Behind the Wheel'?"

He looked at me as a normal tweener would: with abject horror. I could tell that the wheels of his mind were spinning like a hamster on a Habitrail. I knew what he was thinking. It was a combination of, "Why are you talking to me?" mixed with a little bit of, "Please tell me more."

Before Jake could answer, I explained, "'Sleeping Behind the Wheel' is when the driver closes her left eye facing the window on the driver's side. The driver then opens her mouth a little bit just as she would if she'd fallen asleep. You keep your right eye open so you can see perfectly, but the people on your left side don't know that."

As he began shaking his head from side to side, I quickly filled in the final details. "Then, when a car comes up on the left side, it looks like you are driving while sleeping."

Jake said immediately, "No, I've never heard of that."

I ended with a joke, "'Sleeping Behind the Wheel' works great at a stop light like this, but it does not work well if you are a pirate with an eye patch because then you can't see out of either eye! Arrrrrrgh!"

Just then, I saw a car approaching in my rearview mirror and stated excitedly, "Oh, my gosh! Here comes a car. Let me show you right now!"

As the car approached on the left side I sprung my plan into action. Jake squeaked out, "No, Molly!" then slouched down in his seat so it looked like I was the only one in the car.

A few seconds later, he popped his head up just a smidge to see if the people in the other vehicle were looking in our direction. At that moment, I knew we were going to become fast friends.

Lifting and Shifting Relationships with Our Youth

We can support our children in maintaining their state of peaceful and joyful alignment while they are learning life lessons on their journey by sharing moments of spontaneous and simple fun with them and letting them know they are precious and valued.

Many of our children run the gauntlet each day as soon as they arrive at school. They are met with criticism, negativity, and bullying—many times even from the adults in authority as well as from their peers.

If we parents can be the safe harbor these young souls come home to each day, knowing we will always greet them with unconditional love and kindness, it assists them in building their core strength so they can cancel out negative experiences and comments they encounter out in public. Simple, continuous daily acts of love and kindness from us can help them create balance in a world that is constantly bombarding them with negative messages.

The more we are consciously invested, the more quickly we will be able to recognize if something is shifting into or out of alignment as a result of something our children may have encountered that day at school or out in the world.

Special note: This is the last story I wrote before I hit "save" and sent this book off to my editor. Tears splashed upon my keyboard as I typed. I had been made aware, hours earlier, that one of my son's sixteen-year-old high-school classmates had committed suicide and, on this heels of this, I'd heard about the deadly elementary school shooting in Newtown, Connecticut that claimed twenty-six souls, most of them children. It is upon hearing stories such as these that we find our heart wrenched right out of our chest.

I want you to know that we can turn tragedies we experience here on earth into thousands of stories of triumph by learning lessons from these experiences and desiring a positive change within each one of us to help get it right for another soul next time.

Conscious loving means we are the parents of ALL children, not just our own. When we realize we are all connected, our hearts direct us as we move through life building within us the desire to inspire change in the lives of others in a positive way rather than leaving the impact on another in a negative way.

We see all people not just as a body, but as the beautiful soul that lies beneath the skin. Every soul has beautiful colors that represent their essence. If we train the *eye* to ask the *heart* what each person's soul colors are, the illusion of the exterior shell— the skin—melts away to reveal that soul's true beauty. When we gain this profound insight we soon find that all souls are just as important as our own children, our own family, ourselves. This is why it is vital to go in peace and love them all. By doing this we lovingly honor the legacy of all our youth that have left us too soon.

Starting today, make each encounter with your children matter. Whenever they arrive or leave home, offer them at least one positive, truthful comment that contains something you notice about them at that specific moment. Noticing and honoring our children helps us consciously to stay invested in their lives. For example, just as with a spouse, one of the nicest things you can do to kick-start your children's day is to tell them honestly they look nice as they head out the door. This easy, five-second exchange says to your child: "I see you; I notice you; I love you."

Leaving a mark of kindness on the heart of a child is simple:

- Give an honest compliment. For example: "I like your hair today." "Your eyes are beautiful." "That necklace goes great with your outfit."
- Greet your children with a hug and tell them you love them each day as they arrive home.
- Text a spontaneous message that says, "You're a great kid."
- Leave a kind voicemail on a teenager's cell phone.
- Slip notes in your children's backpacks that say, "You are precious to me."

SIMPLE HUMAN TRUTH

One of the nicest things you can do to kick-start your children's day is to tell them honestly they look nice as they head out the door. This easy, five-second exchange says to your child: "I see you; I notice you; I love you."

Connecting with the Disconnected

It is a pure heart that alerts a conscious mind when another soul is in distress. This next story shows how we can make a difference on a moment's notice. In January 2012, I went to a spiritual seminar in downtown Minneapolis with my sister Carolyn. During the seminar, the speaker took questions from the audience on various topics. A woman in the audience raised her hand; the man with the microphone crossed the room and placed it in front of her. Instead of asking the speaker a question, though, the woman made a shocking statement that quieted the room immediately.

With a quivering voice, she confessed, "I have suicidal thoughts. I don't like my life. I can't shake this horrible feeling. It's always with me."

I could feel people around me becoming emotional as they began connecting with the woman's sadness and intense pain. When she was finished she sat down, wiping tears from her eyes.

What happened next surprised even me. A wave of compassion flowed into my heart and my hand popped up. The man with the microphone glided over to me and stuck it in my direction. I said, "I really feel strongly that we should all pray for her together so she can feel connected." I wanted her to know what it felt like to feel connected with love to God, the Universe, Angels, and to other souls.

The speaker paused for a moment, and then obliged me by asking the audience members to please stand. What happened next was absolutely amazing. We all faced the woman and raised our hands, palms out, and sent her love from our hearts while we prayed for her together in silence. All eighty-plus audience members! As I sat down I could see that her friend was now crying too. She looked my way and mouthed the words, "Thank you."

Having a vested interest in other souls unconditionally creates a ripple effect that produces miracles in the lives of those around us. When we help another feel connected to God, it helps us feel more connected too!

Journaling Your Joy and Kindness

One of the biggest things I've learned on my journey is that, regardless of whatever is going on around me or out in the world, I can remain a beacon of light, kindness, and joy. The more love, kindness, and joy I spread around to others, the more I receive in return.

You'll find that this truth applies to you as well, once you begin to take note of it. Try starting a kindness journal. Write down the kind actions and deeds you perform each day while on your journey, as well as stories of kindness that touched your heart. Recording these kind events cements kindness and love in your heart. When you look back over your journal and recall the memories of how you reached out in love to another, the warmth that washes over you is God's way of saying thank you. The Universe is grateful when we do kind things for others. People doing good works are always cherished, for their kind acts help souls learn that compassion reigns.

SIMPLE HUMAN TRUTH
Having a vested interest in other souls unconditionally creates a ripple effect that produces miracles in the lives of those around us.

---

* * *

We can assist another soul with compassionate kindness in feeling more connected to God at any time, especially moments before death. The next chapter will explain how being present for another during the transition-to-the-light process is a wonderful blessing and a beautiful learning experience for all souls involved.

TRANSITION TO THE LIGHT

The butterfly is a traditional symbol of transformation. The spiral is a symbol of change. Here, confetti falling amidst the spirals is a celebration of the beauty of life: ours, and all that accompanies us on the journey and beyond. There is no end to the celebration that happens in the Universe as it looks upon the creation that is humanity and the creations made by humanity. Here, the butterfly symbolizes humankind evolving to its most magnificent state.

Transition to the Light

Angels of highest light and love,
Angels that radiate beams of pure energy
from the heavens above

Please join us and be with us on this very night,
As the soul of our beloved joins you in flight.

We pray that you send this soul embraced
in your lovely wings,
During his journey may he hear harps,
and trumpets and strings.

Too Busy for the Death of a Loved One

If you had the opportunity to ask any person moments before crossing over the two things he or she most wanted out of life, the answer, I believe, would be to love and be loved unconditionally. This is because love is the pure essence of our souls. I had to learn this lesson the hard way by missing out on one of life's precious opportunities to show unconditional love to my grandmother before she transitioned to God's light.

My grandmother, Myrna—I called her Nana—spent her last weeks on earth in a comfortable hospice room at the end of a hospital corridor. I was thirty-three years old at the time, a self-diagnosed workaholic and perfectionist working ten-hour days and raising my daughter Mallory. Other family members visited Nana in the hospital, faithfully spending what time they could with her before her passing. I, on the other hand, was closed minded and believed I was way too busy to take time out for death.

In her prime, my Nana was a woman of integrity, perseverance, and unshakable faith. She was known for having more stamina than women half her age. Each year she would take my siblings and me to events around Minneapolis, including Dayton's eighth-floor Christmas display downtown; ride the bus with us to ball games at the old Met Stadium; and take us to see the animals at the State Fair across town that signaled the end of another Minnesota summer.

The day of my Nana's funeral, I took just a half-day off work and was seated back at my desk in my office promptly by 2 p.m. I had an unwavering determination to keep life functioning based on my standards of normalcy; this meant not taking the time to face grief, death, or mourning, or to veer off my designated work schedule.

My self-inflicted discipline forced me to miss out on the many blessings death allows when we acknowledge it as a part of life. I missed out on the opportunity to say thank you to Nana for a lifetime of memories. To say, "I love you. I'll miss you." I missed out on the chance to say goodbye and tell her she was a wonderful grandmother.

SIMPLE HUMAN TRUTH

When we face our fear of death and slow down our busy lives, we come to realize our relationships are precious, a part of life's foundation. Knowing this fact helps us to understand that death's true purpose is to teach us how to live.

Facing Death with Unconditional Love

It would take more than a decade for me to recognize the importance of being present for others in death. But the Universe has a way of being very clever, very persistent, and very patient. It will continually place messages in front of our eyes until we decide to lift our blinders and see our way to the truth and receive the dispensed wisdom.

As I've mentioned, in late 2006 my father's health began to decline rapidly and this time, I realized the significance of the remaining time I had with him. I had reflected numerous times over the years on the missed opportunity of showing my grandmother compassionate love at the end of her life. I learned this past lesson by absorbing the wisdom without punishing myself. I now understood that this next marker, losing my father, was a lesson for me to embrace and absorb. The lesson? Life is all about relationships and patient, unconditional love. So this time I was going to face death by living and breathing through the process by being present for my father, loving him completely and unconditionally during his remaining months on this earth. I made it a point to make sure my father knew, before he left this world, how truly loved he was and how grateful I was for all the things he taught me.

I recall it as if it were yesterday. My father was in and out of consciousness many times during the days I spent with him at the hospice in Brooklyn Center, Minnesota before his transition to the light. One particularly significant moment came when he opened his eyes and said, "Could you open the door and let those people in?" That one sentence changed my life. It cemented in my mind that there is no *death* as I had been taught since birth. Instead, there is a beautiful energy *transition* that occurs when we leave our physical bodies. God, loved ones who crossed before us, Angels, and Guides are always with us during life, and they are also there to assist us in what I now call the transition-to-the-light process. Knowing this new fact brought joy to my heart as I sat quietly loving my father.

God never leaves His children to wander alone. We are always surrounded with unconditional love. Even if we refuse to see spiritually during our lifetime, the veil between Heaven and earth is much thinner during the life-transition process because we have one foot in each of two worlds, making the connection between these dimensions more accessible.

SIMPLE HUMAN TRUTH

God never leaves His children to wander alone. We are always surrounded with unconditional love.

Moments Before the Transition to the Light

James Hershey, Molly's father: Triathlete, loving Dad, and Grandpa

It had been a very long day at the hospice where my father was living out his remaining hours on earth. Earlier that day, each member of our family had lovingly said goodbye to my father and given him permission to leave this world. We had learned earlier from the compassionate hospice nurses that granting permission to leave eases the soul's ties, releasing the bonds and obligations that may hold the person back from departing freely.

It was now after 10 p.m. My entire family was exhausted, and everyone but me had left for the evening. I was now alone with my thoughts and my father. I had received a very strong and undeniable message, which had popped into my head a few days before. Namely, that I was to stay with him when he crossed over to God's light. I was honored to receive this gift and grateful that I had listened to the spiritual sign instead of discounting it or plowing right past it.

As I sat by his bedside I held his hand and sent him feelings of pure love and gratitude from my heart. I told him he was a wonderful man and a great dad and grandfather. I reassured him that all those relatives who had passed before him would be waiting in God's light with open arms to receive him. To make it even more real, I began to tick off names. I said, "Your sisters Betty and Margaret will be there, your Mom and Dad, your favorite dog Mikey, and most importantly, God."

My father had been a triathlete and running was his passion. So I turned these final moments on earth into the race of his life. I continued, "See that yellow ribbon up ahead? Head toward it, you are almost there. You ran a good race and you fought a good fight and now it's time to break through that ribbon and run into God's beautiful light."

The moment I said that last word, I felt a shift of energy and I knew in my heart that he had heard every single word as spoken. I knew he could feel and hear the absolute truth contained within the final sentences I would speak to him while he was in his physical body.

From previous conversations with my father over the years, I knew he would not want me to see him take his last breath. Honoring wishes or requests is one of the intentional final gifts you can give another soul before he or she leaves this world. So I told him I loved him one last time. Speaking softly and slowly, I said, "I am leaving the room, but not the building. I will be here with you. I am now going down the hall." I picked up my bags noisily so he could hear that I was moving as promised.

Moments later, as I sat in the chair in the waiting room at the end of the hall, a nurse came to tell me she had looked in on my father and that he had just passed away. I got up immediately and headed back into the room; upon entering, I saw another nurse with a stethoscope to his chest.

She announced, "His heart is taking one last flutter here."

I felt so blessed with those eight words, for I had honored my father's wish to not have me see him take his last breath, and he had honored me by allowing me to be in the room with him when he crossed over to God's light.

SIMPLE HUMAN TRUTH

*Honoring wishes or requests is one of the
intentional final gifts you can give another soul
before he or she leaves this world.*

On the Way Home

After saying goodbye to my father for the last time that night, I traveled home alone with my thoughts. I lived thirty-five miles north of Minneapolis at the time, and was on the last leg of my lonely journey back, which covered a twelve-mile stretch of road with only one lane heading north and one lane heading south. I was driving and crying; in between breaths, waiting for my next loud cry to emerge, I heard a voice inside my head. The voice said, "Slow down." I was going 60 mph at the time, and knew right away it was important to pay attention.

I slowed the car down to about 5 mph. As I came around a bend, there, standing in the middle of the road, was a deer. It was beautiful, gentle, and peaceful. Our eyes locked. I stared at the deer and the deer stared back at me through the windshield.

The words came flowing out of my mouth: "I got it Dad, I love you. Thanks for letting me know that you are OK."

At the end of that sentence the deer trotted to the side of the road. As I drove away slowly, the deer remained in my rearview mirror, looking in the direction of my taillights, until the darkness of the night filled in the space between me and the spiritual sign my father and the Universe had sent just for me.

My Mother's Transition

Carolyn Olson and Helen Hershey, Molly's sister
and mother, spreading sunshine

Helping my mother prepare for her transition to the light was also very special and spiritual for me. She was a wonderful role model who loved a lot and learned a lot during her seventy-six years on this earth. She lived life by mastering the art of gratitude. Where others might have complained, blamed, cast judgment, or lived in the past, my mother talked each day about how grateful she was for everything she had. For example, during the end stages of her cancer, she had surgery to place a pin in her arm. When she came out of anesthesia the nurse asked, "How are you feeling?"

My mother replied, "Wonderful, and thank you."

My mother was truly a teacher by demonstration, not preaching. She taught us four kids how to be loving siblings with one another, and how to be friends with one another. She also taught us how to have compassion for others, to show care and concern, to laugh, and to love. She taught us that life is all about relationships, not the material things you must leave behind when you leave this earth. She was a kind and gentle soul and left an impact on many hearts during her precious time here.

Soul Color

Helen Hershey's Soul Drawing by artist Cynthia Shepherd

A few months before my mother's surgery, I met with my friend Cynthia Shepherd for a private spiritual reading. She was in the middle of working on a soul drawing for me when she stopped with a perplexed look on her face and stated, "Wait, this is for your mom." The soul drawing showed a golden color, representing my mother's joyful soul color, and in the upper left-hand corner of the drawing, in the mist, were images that transmitted the feeling of beautiful Angelic presences starting to emerge. These presences let it be known that they would be waiting for her upon her transition to the light. It would not be long.

Creating the Bridge to Heaven
(four weeks before the transition)

I had been visiting with my mother frequently at her apartment before her transition to the light in May 2012, and each time I visited I brought a special book I had found at my local library called *The Complete Encyclopedia of Angels* by Susan Gregg. I felt in my heart that the book would help her process things more easily and allay any fears she might be experiencing. I also wanted to help ease her into feeling a connection with her personal Angels and God.

It was a simple and beautiful book, which described the special gifts of each of the Saints, Archangels, and Ascended Masters (people who have once walked this earth but are now in spirit guiding us from the other side). The book also contained beautiful true stories of healing and some of the teachings of these Ascended Masters. My mother felt an immediate connection to this book and particularly loved the story that involved Ascended Master Mahatma Gandhi.

The story has been retold through the years in many different versions, but the truth of its premise remains the same. The version of this story in this particular book tells of a woman who traveled a great distance to have Gandhi convince her daughter to stop eating sugar. Mahatma Gandhi lived in the truth and by his own teachings. So Gandhi listened very patiently to the woman as she told him about her daughter and her sugar-eating habit. When the woman finished speaking, Gandhi told the mother and daughter simply, "Come back in two weeks."

The woman did as she was told and traveled with her daughter once again a great distance to reach him. Gandhi invited the two to sit. He then looked at the daughter and said, "Stop eating sugar."

The woman became very upset. She asked tersely, "Why couldn't you have told me this two weeks ago?"

Gandhi replied, "Madam, two weeks ago I was still eating sugar."

When I finished reading that story, my mother and I both agreed that it was a perfect example of teaching and living in the truth.

Later that week, after receiving permission from my mother, I brought a friend with me for our visit. My friend connects people with their personal Angels so they can feel the Divine and loving connection to God, the Source of All That Is. We spent an exceptionally powerful hour with my mother that day. She felt the beautiful connection with her Guardian Angel. She also reconnected with my father, who comforted her by saying there would be a celebration upon her arrival. She shed old baggage of the past and granted forgiveness for things that happened thirty-five years earlier. She released, she processed, and she forgave. I left her apartment with a light heart that day because I knew my mother's heart was lighter, too!

Releasing Regrets and the Power of Forgiveness
(three weeks before the transition)

Three weeks before my mother's transition my husband Peter and I went to visit. We had just sat down at her bedside when she said, "I think this is really it this time." She had been on a long, four-year journey of hospital stays, doctor visits, and rehabilitation as her cancer progressed and spread through her body. The recent surgery to repair her broken arm had really begun to take its toll on her physically.

I asked her if she would like to talk about anything she was experiencing or feeling. In a very quiet voice, she said, "I have some regrets."

I said in turn, "Let's make that right, real quick and easy. Let's say a simple prayer for all of us, because Peter and I have regrets and forgiveness we can release, too."

Peter and I each took one of her hands and we formed a prayer circle as my mother lay in her bed.

This is the simple prayer we said together to release, to forgive, and to love:

"I forgive myself.

I forgive all.

I love myself.

I love all.

I release all regrets.

All is released and forgiven.

I am unconditionally loved.

I am washed clean.

I am one of God's children.

Amen."

SIMPLE HUMAN TRUTH
It is through love that the door to Heaven
is opened on earth.

Calling All Angels
(two weeks before the transition)

The final shift came quickly for my mother. My entire family could sense she was getting ready to leave this world. We had been through this just five years earlier with my father, and recognized the signs immediately. We made a call to the hospice center in Brooklyn Center, Minnesota, where my father had spent his last two peaceful weeks on earth—and learned there were no beds available.

So I called on my friends for prayer and my Angels and Guides for assistance. I sent out the request, "Please help us find the perfect location for my mother's transition to the light." By the end of the day, my family and I had found a wonderful new hospice center located in Brooklyn Park, Minnesota, which had opened in February 2012. The location was beautiful, comfortable, and filled with love and light.

The transfer to the hospice center via ambulance took place on a beautiful sunny day in May. As the paramedics closed the door, I called in the Angels once again. I asked them to surround my mother's ambulance and my car with peace and love as we traveled to her new destination. I got in the car and followed closely behind. I could feel the love from this Angelic escort, and once or twice I thought I heard their Angelic wings flapping over the ambulance up ahead.

Spiritual Prayer Circle
(one week before the transition)

One week before my mother's passing, my entire family gathered in her hospice room to show this great woman love. There were fifteen of us present that day. We formed a prayer circle by holding hands, with my mother located at the head of the circle. Those not physically present were mentioned by name to bring their energy into the circle so they could join us in spirit. We surrounded her in a circle of connected love.

As we all held hands in prayer, we took turns and spoke personally and intentionally to let this great woman know how much she meant to each one of us, and all those she had helped along the way. We wanted her to know the positive mark she was leaving on this earth. We were celebrating her accomplished life, and we reassured her that we would persevere once it was time for her to leave. We showered her with love.

Leaving a Kind Legacy

My mother passed away on May 17, one day before her seventy-seventh birthday. When my childhood friend Gail heard of my mother's transition to the light, she sent me an e-mail: "Growing up on our childhood street, your mom was the neighborhood mom. I was at your house just about every day during the summer months, and she made me feel cared about. She was a reassuring figure for me back then."

This e-mail proved to me once again that kindness always leaves a timeless deposit on the heart.

SIMPLE HUMAN TRUTH
Kindness always leaves a timeless deposit on the heart.

One Last Card Game

There are many ways to send a soul to the light with love. My husband Peter had a group of close childhood friends that had kept in touch over the years. One of these friends was a dear man named George. The bond between these great friends spanned the decades, with its roots firmly planted in memories formed during their carefree days of bumming around Milwaukee, Wisconsin, and long nights in smoke-filled rooms playing cards and telling stories.

Whenever Peter had the opportunity to travel back to Milwaukee to visit, he would make it a point to reconnect with George and their close-knit group of friends for a night of playing cards and reminiscing.

In 2008, George was diagnosed with terminal cancer. It was one of those cancers that didn't take no for an answer, and one year later Peter got the call that his dear friend was not doing well.

I clearly remember the conversation I had with Peter that day. He hung up the phone and cried in disbelief. The reality that he would soon be losing this friend of more than forty years was almost too much to bear. We spoke at length and I talked about the importance of being present for George by taking the time to say goodbye before he transitioned to God's light. I suggested that perhaps Peter could organize a "Celebration of Life" card party for his dear friend.

My husband has a heart of gold, and he is an incredible

networker. Over the next few weeks he sent e-mails, made phone calls, and organized a party for George. Two weeks later he flew to Milwaukee for the Celebration of Life card party, attended by all his buddies and the Man of Honor, George.

Peter returned from his visit and recalled with tears in his eyes how each of the guys had shown deep respect in letting George know how much they cherished his friendship. He also told me how each friend had acknowledged and thanked him personally for organizing an event that was so meaningful to George and each person present. Peter's dear friend George passed away one week later.

A Spiritual Thank You

Two days after George passed away, I was at an office-supply store buying ink cartridges for my printer. I happened to look across the store at another register and thought, "My gosh, that man looks just like Peter's friend George." As I looked down to give the store clerk my check card, the man came over from across two rows of registers and stood right next to me in line. I knew this was a spiritual sign, for I have received many similar signs from my father since his passing. I said to myself, "Hey, George."

It is truly incredible how the Universe lines up miracles behind the scenes and, at the perfect moment, allows two people to come together so a spiritual message can be delivered and, we hope, received by the intended party. George knew I would be open to recognizing the spiritual sign, so I could in turn relay the "hello" from George back to Peter.

Our deceased loved ones are never far. If you look, you will see endless signs from those who have transitioned to the light before you. All you have to do is be open to them and there they will be.

Two weeks after I received the first spiritual message from George at the office-supply store, another message was delivered. It was dusk. Peter and I were driving down the highway when a cute old man driving a big old Buick passed us on the right side. As I looked over, I noticed the man had an illuminated, personalized license plate.

I thought to myself, "That is weird. Who has an illuminated license plate?" When I looked more closely, I laughed out loud, for the plate said simply, GEORGE.

I tapped Peter on the shoulder and said, "Look, your friend George is giving you a shout out."

SIMPLE HUMAN TRUTH

Our deceased loved ones are never far. If you look,
you will see endless signs from those who have
transitioned to the light before you. All you have to do
is be open to them and there they will be.

Celebration of Life Party

The purpose of a Celebration of Life party—like the one Peter had for George—is to gather people in a setting of unified love to show the terminally ill person they made a difference during their time on earth, allowing the opportunity for all to say goodbye; share love; allow forgiveness; eliminate or alleviate regret, guilt, anxiety and fear; and provide closure, so the soul can leave this world with no regrets, bearing peace and love in his or her heart. The guests can be anyone the terminally ill loved one would like to include, such as friends, family, neighbors, co-workers, or any soul your loved one feels a connection to or requests.

There are some ground rules for a successful party; being respectful of the loved one's wishes is of the utmost importance. If the terminally ill individual is a private person and declines a party or does not want particular people there, it is important to take note and follow through with that request. If your loved one declines a party altogether, you still have the option of showing love by recording a heartfelt message or sending a caring letter or e-mail. A Celebration of Life party can be held at any time before the transition of a loved one as long as the guest of honor feels well enough to attend. The party's main focus should be on the positive, with a foundation of love, forgiveness, and joy on behalf of a wonderful life.

As you plan:

- Ask the loved one for permission. *Surprise parties are not appropriate for this purpose.*
- Consult the loved one regarding the details surrounding the event: the guest list, the date, the duration, and so on. Do not invite people who are not on the guest list.
- Keep music, television, and voices low to establish a tranquil and peaceful environment.
- Arrange for those not able to attend to participate in other ways, such as via phone or Skype; a written letter or e-mail; or a recorded message or video.

(Please keep in mind the above are just tips. I welcome you to use the ideas that feel right for you and your family.)

Finding a Special Location for the Transition

Besides a Celebration of Life party, another wonderful gift we can give our loved ones is allowing them to transition in a peaceful setting. Whether the transition occurs at home, a hospital, or a hospice, all that is required is a calm, soothing environment focused on helping the loved one to leave this earth peacefully and transition surrounded by compassion.

Truth and Respect During the Transition

It is extremely important to give your loved one the gifts of respect and peace by being truthful at all times during the transition-to-the-light process. During this process your loved one's senses are extremely heightened. Lying increases fear and agitation. Because of this, a great growth opportunity is available for all souls to speak only the truth.

You can recognize when someone is lying to the dying; they say things like:

- "You are going to be OK."
- "You are going to go to sleep for just a little bit."
- "We aren't going to sell your house."
- "Everything will stay just the same."

It is also untruthful to tell the dying person that someone is coming to say goodbye when you know that person isn't, or aren't sure if he or she will be able to make it.

How to Be Present for Another Soul During the Transition-to-the-Light Process

There are many ways you can show love with simplicity during this time:

- Let him know how much he touched your life.
- Let her know how much you love her.
- Let him know it's OK to transition when he is ready.
- Let her know you and your family members will miss her, but you will persevere after she leaves her physical body.
- Be honest in your words, thoughts, and actions.
- Share stories and memories.
- Ask if there is anyone he would like to say goodbye to.
- Make her as comfortable as possible regarding setting, location, and noise level.
- Speak kindly and softly in his presence.
- Respect her wishes.

Asking Important Questions

As you spend time with and speak honestly with your loved one, clarify final wishes regarding the details surrounding the funeral. These questions may sound strange and feel a bit uncomfortable, but they are necessary to ask in order to fulfill your loved one's final requests. For example, my father, mother, and grandmother were very clear that they wanted to have a closed-casket funeral, and my family respected their wishes.

While he or she can still communicate, ask your loved one:

- "Do you want family members in the room with you

during the transition to God's light? If so, which specific family members would you like by your side?"
- "Do you want a small, intimate funeral or memorial service, or a large one?"
- "Do you want an open or closed casket, or would you like to be cremated?"
- "Are there specific songs you would like included in the service?"
- "Is there a specific poem or reading that has special meaning to you that should be included?"
- Do you have a specific person you would like to deliver the service and the eulogy?"

Transition to the Light: Stages

Part of being present for your loved ones as they are preparing to leave the physical body is understanding the process they are undergoing, so you can assist them through it. The stages of this process include:
- Fear surrounding the transition to the light
- Processing—thoughts, feelings, and dreams
- Reconciliation and forgiveness
- One foot in both worlds / getting ready to travel
- Permission to leave
- Sensitivity
- Transition to the light

DISPELLING THE FEAR SURROUNDING TRANSITION TO THE LIGHT

During this process eliminate fear by talking about the process without any kind of emotional charge. When my father was ill, we did a lot of things right, but we also avoided having conversations with him regarding the fact that he was actively in the transitioning process and would soon be crossing over to God's light. A simple, five-minute conversation can open the door for more thought and dialogue the next time you visit. Peace, love, and truth reside in open communication. Fear becomes the ruler when thoughts remain locked behind the doors of our minds.

STARTING A DIALOGUE FOR PROCESSING THOUGHTS, FEELINGS, AND DREAMS

Many times, before our loved ones transition to the light, a deceased relative or an Angel or Guide comes to them in dreams to work with their subconscious mind in order to ease the transition. Talking to a loved one about some of the things they are experiencing can help them gain insight and peace during this process.

A simple series of questions can start the necessary dialogue comfortably:

- "Is there anything you would like insight on regarding what you are experiencing?"
- "Do you want to talk about any thoughts, feelings, or dreams?"
- "Can I explain to you what I have heard happens during the process of transition to God's light?"

RECONCILIATION AND FORGIVENESS

Ask your loved one if there is anyone they feel they need to forgive, reconcile with, or say goodbye to. Assisting a loved one in leaving this world and sending them to God's light with love, a forgiving heart, and no regrets is one of the biggest spiritual gifts you can bestow.

Here are some ideas:

- Offer to guide your loved one through a simple prayer of forgiveness as found in the earlier section of this chapter (*Releasing Regrets and the Power of Forgiveness*).
- Offer to organize a Celebration of Life Party providing the opportunity to gain closure with multiple people at once.
- Explain why heart-centered forgiveness allows for purity in its release, allowing for a peaceful transition with no regrets.

ONE FOOT IN BOTH WORLDS/
GETTING READY TO TRAVEL

Our loved ones show us many spiritual signs in the days and hours leading up to the time their spirit/soul is preparing to travel. All you have to do is be alert and look for the signs.

Both my father and mother were very busy in the days leading up to their transition to the light. They were seeing and speaking to friends and relatives who had passed before them. While in and out of consciousness, my mother talked about traveling on the bus and making sure she paid off a past debt. My father said he wanted to make sure his cell phone was charged and his train tickets were purchased. From his bed, in his dreams, he was reliving riding his prized Indian motorcycle as he had back in the 1950s, making motions in the air with his arms and hands such as cupping his palms and swiveling his wrists back and forth.

Each spiritual sign is a gift not to be forgotten. Keep a notebook in the room so family members can record the date, time, and details of significant moments, comments, or conversations with your loved one during the transitioning process. As you look upon this notebook after the transition to the light, you will find that many of the events recorded will hold special meaning for family members, friends, relatives, and co-workers. This notebook can then become a spiritual keepsake or diary, with significant markers containing poignant details and wonderful memories.

GRANTING PERMISSION TO LEAVE

Parents may feel the need to hold on longer than necessary in this world because of the caretaker role they have held within the family unit. This feeling of responsibility, holding everything together, is very powerful and can prolong the process of transition to the light. Verbally giving our loved ones permission to leave and letting them know truthfully that you will be all right after they transition allows for a more peaceful release.

If the one transitioning is a terminally ill child, it's very important to tell him or her that mom and dad are going to be OK. You will never forget them. You will really miss them, but you are going to keep moving forward one step at a time and one day at a time. You can help young children transition to the light peacefully by telling them truthfully that you will always keep them close to your heart, but will not hold them back from going to God.

ACKNOWLEDGING SENSITIVITY

Hearing, sight, and skin sensitivity are most acute before the transition. Speaking kind words softly and lightly and gently touching your loved one without rubbing the skin is a wonderful way to show your presence without creating irritation. Diffused lighting is preferable to fluorescent lighting. Bringing in a lamp from home can lessen harsh lighting and create a more comfortable atmosphere.

I also believe that even if their eyes are closed, our loved ones can pick up on the body language and emotions of others present. Before you enter the room, take a moment to move your attention consciously from your head down to your heart space. Ask the visiting guests to do the same. This process will allow you to emit the energy of unconditional love instead of worry, fear, or sadness.

TRANSITIONING TO THE LIGHT

Think of our human body as a butterfly's chrysalis. When it is time to leave this earth, the chrysalis (body) opens and a beautiful butterfly (spirit) emerges. When we shed our earthly body, our spirit connects with our soul and is transported back to Source—God. Transition to the light is a part of life. Have peace in knowing, dear ones, that we are all composed of energy. Energy never dies. It is always changing and transforming.

As stated earlier, it is vital to have a dialogue early on to assist a loved one in determining if they would like anyone in the room with them during the actual transition. When the time draws near we can still be present for a love one in spirit, even if we are not in the same room, the same state, or even the same country simply by holding thoughts of peace for the person and sending love from our hearts. This is possible because we are all one. We are all energy.

If you are with a loved one who is moments from transitioning to the light and wish to send him or her to God with peace and love, a simple final statement could go like this: "I am sending you love from my heart. We will remain connected at the soul level always. Go in peace, for you are dearly loved by me and the heavens."

SIMPLE HUMAN TRUTH
*Have peace in knowing, dear ones, that we are
all composed of energy. Energy never dies.
It is always changing and transforming.*

Celebration of Life Funeral or Memorial Service

Once the loved one has transitioned, there will usually be a funeral or memorial service. Consider a Celebration of Life service similar to a Celebration of Life party. The focus now will be on the beauty of the soul's journey and capturing the impact that soul left on this earth during a wonderful life. Presenting uplifting music, pictures, videos, and poems and shared inspirational stories about the loved one are all great ways to help other souls carry lasting memories in their hearts of the soul who has passed before them.

SIMPLE HUMAN TRUTH
Love is fuel for the soul.

Being Present for Others After the Transition to the Light

After my father's and mother's transitions to the light, it meant the world to me when people showed support by being present at the funeral service or wake. Even if a guest could stop by for only a moment, it was wonderful to feel that kind of connected love and support.

The kindness sent from one compassionate soul to another during the time of loss of one held so dear allows the sorrow-filled heart to open wide, filling the space of emptiness that grief may have created with a renewed sense of peace, compassion, and love.

This is why, two years after my father's transition to the light, I made it a point to attend services for the late fathers of two separate real estate clients. Each time, I received confirmation of how much it means to another soul when we show compassion and love. On one such occasion, when my client saw me enter the room, she exclaimed, "Molly's here! Molly, thank you so much for coming!"

She then went on to introduce me to her family and friends by saying, "This is Molly, my friend." She didn't introduce me as "Molly, my Realtor," but as "Molly, my friend." I knew then that my act of compassion had made a difference.

SIMPLE HUMAN TRUTH

The kindness sent from one compassionate soul to another during the time of loss of one held so dear allows the sorrow-filled heart to open wide, filling the space of emptiness that grief may have created with a renewed sense of peace, compassion, and love.

---

* * *

By embracing my initial fear of death, I received an incredible gift and came to the knowing that we are all divinely connected and that when we take our last breath on earth, it is to the same Source of energy in light we return. When our soul transitions to the light, we return to the pure essence of love. The next chapter will show you how to return to your own loving essence through the process of finding pure truth while you still walk upon this earth.

Truth

EVERY SOUL DESERVES THE TRUTH

Truth is meant to be at the center of all our relationships. With truth at the center, our relationships grow rich and strong and flow us bountiful blessings. We appreciate all the vibrant colors of life. We need to keep all the parts of us in balance and in sync with truth or our relationships are like a chair with wobbly legs; it won't take much to knock us off balance. Being truthful is one of the ways we love, and true love cannot exist if truth is absent. Making sure that all the quadrants of our being have truth at their center ensures authentic, rich relationships.

Every Soul
Deserves the Truth

*TRUTH serves a great purpose for all that want to see.
It will help uncover your life's mission in order to reveal
what your soul wants you to be.*

Truth

There is special significance and a truth to be revealed in absolutely everything we do, even something as simple as purchasing an item—like this book—in a store or online. A subtle shifting occurred behind the scenes to get us to that precise point in time. The sooner we come to understand Divine Synchronicity, the sooner we come to know that nothing is insignificant and there are no coincidences.

God, our Spirit Guides, and Angels are guiding us with unconditional love, truth, and wisdom continuously behind the scenes, steering us in the specific direction our souls want us to travel. Once our spirit here, in this human body, decides to become illuminated, the truths that have always been presented to us in the form of synchronicities become more and more apparent in our everyday tasks, encounters, and events.

We begin to say things like, "Why didn't I see that before?" We begin to recall occurrences that passed by us without our giving them much thought, but that are now being brought forth in the form of reflection for optimal learning. We begin to know that everything is divinely connected and divinely guided.

Picking up a book that feels right to you at a specific time in your life is part of a Divine Illumination puzzle piece locking into its Divine Place. As your desire to live in the truth builds, your ability to see the truth in the synchronicities placed before you will build, too!

Harold the Turkey Totem

"Peeping Tom" shows up for the first time, September 2009

Harold the Turkey Totem returns, February 2010

Synchronicities can come in many forms, some of them quite quirky. It was right around my birthday in September 2009 when Harold showed up for the first time. I was working in my home office, which looks out over a wooded area at the back of our house. I was sitting at my desk with my back to the sliding glass doors that lead to the deck when I heard a *tap, tap, tap* behind me. I turned to see what was making the noise and there, staring at me through the other side of the glass, was a male turkey. The first thing that popped into my head was, "So this is what it's like to have a Peeping Tom in the neighborhood." I laughed at the silliness of it all, took a few pictures of this fowl fella, and went back to work without much thought.

I have found my Angels and Spirit Guides have a wonderful sense of humor and a very patient way of repeatedly delivering divinely orchestrated synchronistic messages until I absorb the wisdom I am supposed to gain from these spiritual encounters. And what do you know but five months later, on a cold, ordinary day in February, I got up early as usual, poured my cup of coffee, and looked out the dining room window. There, perched on our deck railing, was another enormous male turkey.

I thought to myself, "Could this be the same turkey that tapped on my window five months ago?"

I showed each family member the turkey just as they awoke that morning and wiped the sleep from their eyes. We all thought this turkey was pretty cool. So cool, in fact, that we named him Harold.

Harold stayed on our deck railing for an entire week. He never left his perch. It even snowed on top of him one night and when we awoke the next morning he was covered in a blanket of fluffy white snow.

Everyone had an opinion. One friend said, "He must be sick. Turkeys just don't stick around like that."

An avid hunter I knew had a stern warning: "Male turkeys are mean. You'd better stay away from him!"

My mother was the voice of reason, who said in her gentle way, "I think he must know it is safe for him to be at your house."

That statement triggered something in me. A light bulb went off in my head. "Duh," I thought, as I finally connected the dots. Harold's return and the duration of his visit told me there was a very spiritually significant message contained within each one of these encounters. This realization prompted me to search the web for information on the meaning of animal totems.

Here is what I found.

Turkey Totem:

Harvest time, makes us thankful for all blessings, shows adaptability in all areas of life, energy of sharing and gift giving, teaches us how to harvest items with patience. It is time to listen to your higher vision to achieve goals, whether spiritual, physical, mental, or emotional. The turkey is the symbol of sacrifice. It gives life so others may live. With a turkey totem, you have transcended self. You act and react on behalf of others with a deep knowledge that all life is sacred. Through giving to others you will reach your own goals.

I was amazed when I found the information about Harold, my turkey totem, for this message had direct and significant meaning for me at that specific time in my life. I have always felt that life is all about relationships and each relationship is of sacred importance, and ironically, when Harold showed up I had been working through learning about all the different facets of patient love.

The Synchronistic Plate

The license plate 888, shown as the 888ᵗʰ picture on Molly's phone

Spiritual synchronicities are often put in place to teach us lessons, give us information, or let us know we are on the right track. It can be enlightening and useful (not to mention fun) when you share your spiritual synchronicity stories with another.

Cynthia Shepherd, the artist who illustrated this book, as I mentioned before, is one of my great friends. We experienced synchronicity after synchronicity while collaborating on this project, sharing them as they happened. Not only was this exchange incredibly fun, but also it kept us motivated and let us know we were heading in the right direction with our thoughts, actions, and concepts.

One particularly amazing synchronicity came in the form of a license plate. Cynthia and I had been following our intuition to develop the concepts for the spiritual artwork at the beginning of each chapter. I had just arrived at the library parking lot and looked at the car parked across from me as I exited my own. The license plate read 888, followed by some letters. I felt what I call a "zinger" of electricity run through my body when I saw this plate, one of my personal signals that something significant is before me. So I took a picture of the plate with my cell phone and immediately texted it to Cynthia asking if she knew the spiritual meaning of the number 8.

She texted back, "The receipt of meaningful, revealing, and significant revelations." I read the text and then looked at the picture again on my phone. I couldn't believe what I saw next. The photo I took of the 888 license plate just happened to show on my screen as the 888th photo on my phone. My friend Bonny chimed in later when I told her the story and said, "That is so cool! Multiple eights mean power and abundance."

This is why living in the truth is so wonderful. Once-in-a-lifetime spiritual synchronicities begin to show up as daily events of illumination in our lives.

Every Soul Deserves the Truth

The reason synchronicities occur is to illuminate the way to Divine Truth, even if it's about something we might not want to know but need to acknowledge and absorb for our soul's growth. One of the most memorable experiences flowed to me to help me realize that all souls deserve the truth occurred after meeting a woman named Pam at a seminar back in January 2011. My friend and I had an open spot available at our restaurant booth during lunch break, and we asked Pam if she would like to join us.

As Pam sat down, I initiated the conversation with my table-mates to see how they felt about the importance of telling the truth to others. I was explaining why I believe every soul deserves the truth, every time, regardless of the situation. Pam said, "I have a story for you." She began to tell us that she has premonitions and can see events unfold in the future. Pam recalled a woman she was acquainted with who suffered from severe depression. She said that she could clearly see in her mind's eye the woman taking a gun and shooting herself.

I gasped and asked Pam, "Did you talk to her about your premonition?"

Pam quickly replied, "No. What are you supposed to do with information like that?"

I replied from my heart, "I believe every soul deserves to hear the truth. Telling the truth in a situation like that could have been softened so the blow wouldn't be so harsh and shocking. A softened, yet truthful delivery could have sounded something like this: 'I know this sounds strange, but I feel every soul deserves to hear the truth. I have premonitions. You may not believe this, but I had a vision of you injuring yourself, possibly fatally, in the future and I want you to know that you are loved and people are always available to help you. We are all here to help each other. I believe life is a journey. Is there anything I can do to help you find more joy on your journey?'"

This succinct and truthful statement could have been just what the other woman needed to hear in order to snap her spirit into motion and realize she was not alone.

We continued our conversation and I finished by asking Pam, "Did anything ever happen to her?"

She replied apprehensively. "Yes, she shot herself in the chest but, thank God, she lived."

Speaking the truth to another, whether or not it is difficult to dispense and whether or not the recipient hears it at the time, always shows pure love to another soul. When we withhold the truth from another soul, we miss out on the opportunity to show true love and support.

When a Soul Steps Forward

Our souls and the souls of others constantly step forward to give others clues about something we are experiencing and process-ing in the form of a Spiritual S.O.S. (*Save Our Souls*). This S.O.S. allows another soul the opportunity to offer us wisdom, kindness, or gentle guidance back onto the path of truthful alignment.

Have you ever heard someone say, "I am so weak. I know I am going to fall and break my hip one of these days?" And sure enough, within days, this person falls and breaks a hip. Or perhaps someone else has said, "This job is stressing me out!" And three months later, that person suffers a stress-induced heart attack.

When a soul steps forward in our presence with information contained in the foreshadowing of a future event via speech, actions, premonitions, or dreams, we can be completely present and truthful. It offers an opportunity to make a difference in the life of another by lovingly shining a light on something this person may not be consciously aware of at the time. When we take the time to gently correct another soul who has veered off track and face the situation with love and truth, that soul has the oppor-tunity to realize the connection to all that is. A gentle correction contained within a heartfelt message tells a soul, "I see you; I hear you; I care about you; I love you."

True love for another says, "I shall not discount you by eliminating the truth. I will show you I value you by being completely present and speaking only the truth."

SIMPLE HUMAN TRUTH

When we take the time to gently correct another soul who has veered off track and face the situation with love and truth, that soul has the opportunity to realize the connection to all that is.

Honesty and Integrity Go Hand in Hand

An honest person speaks the truth and lives in truth. When we live in the truth, we are the people another soul can trust implicitly. Our word is our bond. An honest person is the rock another soul can return to in times of need, because they can always be trusted to be there for us. A truly honest person is the type of individual we want to do business with, and to have running our country, taking care of us during critical surgery, watching over our children, and assisting our elderly parents in a nursing home.

Being a person of integrity means we are the same person in all situations and with all people regardless of who is involved, how much money is at stake, and whether or not anyone is watching our behavior. Integrity is being our *authentic self* at all times. Integrity is the sentry of the conscious soul.

Integrity holds the soul's desire for purity in its vibrational field. In this place, we can be a steady and unwavering model for doing what's right. While others may vacillate between honesty and dishonesty, the person of integrity will always choose honesty and becomes a torchbearer of God's light.

I believe we cannot have complete integrity without honesty and we are not an honest person if we lack integrity. Once we have both of these important pieces locked into our sparkling soul puzzle, we are afforded a stronger connection with our Source, our Creator. We become illuminated vessels, fully aware we are the Lightworkers and difference makers, here at this very moment in time to help others awaken the flame contained within and spread God's light throughout the world.

Honesty is powerful and a catalyst for:

- Keeping the light shining from within
- Transformation
- Freedom and liberation
- Simple living
- Peace in relationships

SIMPLE HUMAN TRUTH
Integrity is the sentry of the conscious soul.

Open-Book Living

When we live our life as if it is an open book, we are free in body, mind, and spirit and allow anyone to read from our pages. This is how it feels to live with honesty and integrity. There is nothing to be withheld. There is no information to hide or lock away. When our life is a public record, honesty is natural. Living like this is incredibly liberating.

Open-book living says we are spiritually conscious of:

- The video games we allow into our homes
- The things we watch on television
- The lyrics of the music we listen to
- The websites we visit on our computer
- The lives that may be harmed because of products we purchase
- The behavior we exhibit when no one is watching
- The business establishments we frequent
- The people with whom we choose to surround ourselves as our base relationships
- The way we treat all souls

Living openly and with integrity means we are constantly calibrating our moral compass.

To help yourself do this, answer these questions:

- Is there a behavior that I do only when no one is looking?
- Do I have secrets that I keep from my co-workers, friends, and/or family members?
- Am I cheating on someone or cheating someone out of something?
- Am I a person who does not take the truth seriously?

SIMPLE HUMAN TRUTH
*When we live our life as if it is an open book,
we are free in body, mind, and spirit and allow
anyone to read from our pages.*

Golden Rule Living

*The Golden Rule:
Do unto others as you would have them do unto you.*

Golden Rule Living assists us in making all of our actions personal and keeps us in the right relationship with others. If we are not certain about the integrity of one of our actions, we can simply turn any situation or conversation around by putting ourselves on the receiving end.

Golden Rule Living places us in the position to honor all relationships, including those with:

- Colleagues
- Family
- Friends
- Strangers and acquaintances (*all souls*)

Golden Rule Living:

- Assists us in making our actions personal
- Keeps our integrity in check
- Maintains, promotes, and values precious relationships

The Souls in Our Shoes

Golden Rule Living is the great simplifier. It places us in another soul's shoes, taking what can appear to be a complex decision that involves another and streamlining it to a one-step process of deciding, "If I wouldn't like this done to me, then I shall not do it to another."

Taking this step allows our soul to pause so we can make a divinely correct decision. The Golden Rule can be used to calibrate our moral compass and keep us on the right track every time.

Consider the following examples. Please answer the questions below honestly:

- If you are considering cheating on your test at college, would you want a doctor who cheated on his tests and lied to his professors in medical school to perform your upcoming open-heart surgery?
- If you view pornography of any kind, would you want someone else who views pornography to coach your child's soccer team or take care of your child in an unsupervised daycare setting?
- If you lie repeatedly to others, would you want a person who consistently tells untruths to be your partner in a new business venture or entrusted with your confidential financial business information?

Changing our behavior first, in any situation, can assist us in changing society's behavior.

SIMPLE HUMAN TRUTH
Golden Rule Living is the great simplifier. It places us in another soul's shoes, taking what can appear to be a complex decision that involves another and streamlining it to a one-step process of deciding, "If I wouldn't like this done to me, then I shall not do it to another.

The Truth Holds No Negative Secrets

When we are living an open-book life and following the Golden Rule, there is no place for secrets. This truth struck me as I was sitting in a coffee shop writing this book. A few tables away, two women were having a conversation at a normal volume for about thirty minutes. My clue that a juicy secret about someone not present was about to be told was when one of the women looked around, lowered her voice, and then leaned in to the other woman to give her a bit of information.

To identify a negative secret, look for words like these:

- "Don't tell anybody else."
- "It's our little secret."
- "What they don't know won't hurt them."

If someone should ask you to hold a negative secret, you can simply and honestly say, "I have begun a positive mission to walk in the truth, and an integral part of that is to hold no negative secrets for anyone."

If someone should ask you to hold a positive secret, such as a surprise birthday party or the contents of a holiday gift, you may do so because it does not hold a negative energy vibration.

Holding a Soul in a Positive Light

When we are truly loving all souls, all souls are welcome to hear what we have to say—anywhere, any place, and at any time. We speak no ill of another. We have no secrets and we ask no one to *hold the energy* of a negative secret for us. We have shifted from living from our heads to living from our Divine Hearts. A Divine Heart, once awakened, will always place another soul in a pillar of white light of positivity and unconditional love. Holding a soul in this beautiful space magnifies our love and pure intent.

The Truth Demands Progress and Change

Secrets of any kind can destroy trust in relationships. The negative energy, if allowed to grow, can turn into the withholding of a truth that is so vital that it grows into a dramatic event that may even turn into an epic disaster.

While writing this book, I had drinks one evening with my good friend Cindy. She began the conversation with a very poignant and truthful statement that helped me see another reason why the truth is so vital for growth.

Cindy began, "Molly, think of this aspect regarding truth. Sometimes it's just easier to lie, because truth many times demands progress and change. And, to be quite honest, many times people don't like change because change is difficult."

I replied, "That is a great point. I do believe that for many, it is easier to lie on the front end. It's the cleanup from the drama the lie created on the back end that is not so easy. Major oil spills in history have demonstrated this important lesson."

Change is good. Change is progress. Change is growth. Change is inevitable. Not telling the truth to a deserving party is part of the illusion that lying is easier. I have come to know from my own life lessons that lying to another is anything but a time saver. It demands additional time; first, for the resulting drama once the lie is revealed and then, for the work necessary to clean up and repair the damage the lie does to our precious relationships or, in the case of an actual oil spill, our environment.

Truth demands progress and change, and is always for the benefit of all souls—even if you must travel through a difficult learning process or make a shift as a result of facing the truth. The end result of the learning shift is always a simpler and cleaner way of life.

Truth sets in motion many wonderful things:

- It moves you into your heart space, where love resides.
- It ensures you are doing your part to grow your soul.
- It helps you to be in the right relationship with all souls.
- It raises your joy vibration.
- It helps you to release the ego and self-centeredness, so you become as invested in others as you are in yourself.
- It helps you to process information faster.
- It breaks through all illusions.
- It helps you find and fulfill your purpose for this lifetime.

SIMPLE HUMAN TRUTH

Truth demands progress and change, and is always for the benefit of all souls—even if you must travel through a difficult learning process or make a shift as a result of facing the truth.

Telling the Truth to Our Children

Living in the truth allows us to honor our words and value those to whom we are connected. On Christmas Eve 2011, my husband, all four of our children, Hailey, and I were on our way to church, traveling in two cars. Peter was traveling in the lead car with Will, Jake, and Maddy. Mallory, Hailey, and I followed in the car behind.

Up ahead I noticed a police car in the middle of the road, lights flashing. My husband's car slowed down and passed the police car on the right. We immediately mirrored his behavior. As we passed the police car, my daughter and I noticed a black dog lying in the road.

My granddaughter asked from the backseat, "Grandma, is that a dog in the road?"

I replied, "Yes, Hailey, it is. Could you please say a prayer for the dog?"

Hailey immediately said, "Dear Lord, please watch over this dog for all of us. Amen."

I said. "Thank you for caring for one of God's creatures. That was really nice."

When we arrived home from the Christmas Eve service that night, twenty-one-year-old Maddy asked, "Was that a dog in the road on the way to church?"

I said. "Yes, it was a dog. Hailey said a prayer for it when we drove by." Maddy replied, "I knew it! Dad said it was a raccoon."

I circled back around to my husband the next day and asked kindly, "Why didn't you tell the truth to Maddy about the dog in the road?"

Peter replied, "I didn't want the drama surrounding her being upset about a dog being hit."

I said truthfully, "Honey, the drama you were trying to avoid by not telling the truth actually created drama."

Two separate cars. One identical scene. Two different results.

One car: Untruth = drama.

Another car: Truth = prayer.

When children see the adults in their lives happy and peaceful, speaking kind words and loving each other by holding each other accountable, they come to understand that love and truth make all things right.

Our children deserve the truth regardless of their age. Telling children the truth has many benefits:

- When we speak respectfully about others in the presence of our children, we role model truly loving behavior.
- When we keep our promises and honor our words, we treat our children with respect.
- When adults role-model integrity, children feel secure.

SIMPLE HUMAN TRUTH

When children see the adults in their lives happy and peaceful, speaking kind words and loving each other by holding each other accountable, they come to understand that love and truth make all things right.

Avoiding Drama

Staying current. Staying truthful. Staying kind. These are the three main ways we can remain in the correct, peaceful alignment with all souls who enter or leave our presence. Facing any situation with peace and love brings anything that may need immediate alignment out into the light for easiest resolution. When truthful knowledge is dispensed, soul growth is accomplished every time, for all parties involved, in every situation.

Drama can be avoided by:

- Staying current on all conversations
- Setting boundaries and clear expectations
- Providing and presenting all factual information
- Never assuming anything
- Having all souls involved in the situation present during the resolution discussion
- Speaking truthfully about how you feel at the time the event occurs
- Speaking no ill behind someone's back
- Holding all souls accountable for their behavior with love
- Treating all parties with respect
- Redirecting conversations back to the truth
- Avoiding dredging up situations from the past that have no bearing on the current issue at hand

---

SIMPLE HUMAN TRUTH
When truthful knowledge is dispensed,
soul growth is accomplished every time,
for all parties involved, in every situation.

***

Once we understand why every soul deserves the truth, we can take the next step, which is illuminating societal illusions by shining the light on untruthful patterns so we can break free of them.

ILLUMINATING WHAT'S BEHIND THE CURTAIN

The Phoenix stands for renewal, transformation and rebirth, but it is also a symbol of the light of truth, depth of spiritual awareness, and purity. Phoenix represents the soul's call for right alignment in our lives and for us to return to the pure state we were in at the time of our birth into this world, when our intentions were pure and our wisdom was whole. It is also about surrender; as the Phoenix surrenders to the flames that consume it—knowing that it will be resurrected—so, too, must we surrender our fears of the unknown and know that we are loved and supported in our journey so that we can be the embodiment of the fullest expressions of peace, joy, love, and truth.

Illuminating What's Behind the Curtain

A person can put up any kind of protective wall,
but love and truth always find a way around it.

Love and Truth Break Through Illusions

My good friend Bonny Kraus, a teacher and healer, works with the energy of the Angels as a powerful tool. Part of her healing practice involves receiving messages of love for her clients from the Angels, which are called channeled Angel messages. In October 2012, I invited Bonny to be a guest on the Violet Wisdom Inspiration Radio show. We dedicated an entire hour to a discussion on breaking through illusions.

On the show that day, Bonny and I discussed the importance of linking our hearts to the heavens, which allows us to form a connected partnership with the Divine. Once we make the conscious effort to stay connected in this way, we come to know through love and truth that the Universe has our back at all times. We also come to know that our Angels and Guides are constantly orchestrating, guiding, and directing us with this love behind the scenes.

Knowing these facts helps us to arrive at a new stop on our journey where we are comfortable enough to pack up the illusions of fear and worry by handing that baggage over to the Divine, allowing for a peaceful release from these negative emotions and the arrival of joy in our daily lives.

Bonny cemented this truth for our listeners by eloquently explaining that unconditional love contains no fear or worry. She said, "Many of us grew up in conditional love families, conditional love religions, and conditional love situations. Once we can let go of our past, we can move into the knowledge that anything based in pain, suffering, struggle, conditional love, or fear is an illusion."

Bonny then asked me if it would be all right to channel directly a message regarding truth and love from the Archangel Raphael, and I agreed.

Here is an excerpt from that message:

> *Unconditional love is all that's real. Joy is all that's real. The places that have no opposites are all that's real, and these are the choices that we can make here, now, as we move into the consciousness of the new world of victory.*
>
> *We move from victim consciousness, which does not exist—it is the illusion—to victory consciousness. We move from lack consciousness, which is not the truth. And we move into prosperity consciousness. We move from that place of doubt, fear, and distrust into trusting every moment that everything is in Divine Order. We move from that conditional love that says, 'If you do this, then I'll love you. If you act that way, then I'll love you.' And all those conditions we were taught we had to do in order to get to Heaven.*
>
> *We allow those to just melt away and we see them just running off the sides of our energy fields like butter as we reclaim on the deepest levels of our heart center the unconditional*

love of our true self. And that is all that matters; that is the place beyond the illusion.

We can know this simple human truth after receiving this powerful message channeled from Archangel Raphael. Fear has no place in the lives of those who choose to be victorious.

SIMPLE HUMAN TRUTH
Fear has no place in the lives of those who choose to be victorious.

Illuminators

Illuminators are the people who shine a light on long-held beliefs, policies, patterns, societal "shoulds," and illusions. They have the power to illuminate the truth with love, allowing others to remove their blinders, thus affording souls the option to turn within and find their own truth and inner voices. These souls, with their new vision, can also become difference makers who go on to help others and start a movement of change in the world for the better.

Illuminators are souls who light the path for other souls. These are the people that lend an ear, give a hand, and offer a shoulder to cry on. They teach instead of preach. They may touch the life of just one soul at a time, or they may light the path for many.

You can become an Illuminator. All you need to do is work on yourself first, then develop equal care and concern for fellow souls, blessing others by shining the light of pure truth from your heart for all to see.

What's Behind the Curtain?

We can become an Illuminator and make a difference by kindly illuminating an illusion when we see someone perform any action that is out of alignment with the truth in our presence. In the movie *The Wizard of Oz*, Dorothy's dog Toto became an Illuminator when he drew back the curtain to reveal a frightened little man deceiving others into believing he was the Great Oz. Deception can only live in the darkness and shadows. There is no place for it to hide once it is illuminated.

Once the truth was kindly revealed to Dorothy, she was able to take her blinders off, see the light, and understand she needed to use discernment and know the truth instead of giving away her power to someone who was deceiving her. When Dorothy became illuminated, she switched on her own inner truth. The wisdom that flowed in behind the illumination allowed her the insight to make her own correct decisions regarding which path to take in order to return home safely. She realized that this truth had been with her all along.

SIMPLE HUMAN TRUTH
Deception can only live in the darkness and shadows. There is no place for it to hide once it is illuminated.

Societal Illusions

Remaining in a state of peace, joy, love, and truth is vital for pulling back the curtain on the illusions of this world and dismissing the false grip each illusion has had on our selves and on our society.

Some of the main illusions include:

deception	victimization
cheating	anger
stealing	murder
adultery	fear
pornography	addictions
slander	hatred
separation from God	slavery and human trafficking

Identifying illusions is a matter of checking in with our gut intuition and our pure heart in order to register how we are feeling at any moment and thus receiving the gift of pure sight. We can *pull back our own curtain*. If we feel that we have shifted out of alignment and are not in a state of peace, joy and love, we know that we have traveled from our truth and that something needs loving attention and correction.

We can distinguish between truth and illusion by asking two simple questions:
- Does this action or feeling have love as its foundation?
- Does this action or feeling occur in Heaven?

If the answer is no, then we can be assured it is an illusion.

*"You may use my sword to cut
through any illusion of fear."*

—Molly Friedenfeld's channeled message from Archangel Michael

A Kink in My Hose

In the illumination process it is important also to point out the reactions caused by our untruthful actions. Illuminating what we don't want can help us to build the desire for what our souls do want—truth. Have you ever tried to water your garden while there is a kink in the hose? It presents quite a challenge, restricting the flow of life-giving water or stopping it altogether. The telling of untruths does the same thing: It restricts the flow of love to the other precious souls in our lives, who deserve to feel unrestricted love from our pure hearts.

When my hose gets a kink, many times I have been lazy about fixing it. Instead of traveling directly to the kink and removing the blockage immediately, with both hands, I attempt to correct it from a distance by snapping the hose from where I stand. Most times, the frustrating kink stays right where it is and the flow of water remains restricted. Similarly, each time we tell an untruth, we create drama and restrict the flow of love. If we travel to the restriction immediately, we can correct the problem and restart the flow of love and truth.

What happens when we tell an untruth?

- It hurts and negatively affects those we love most.
- It stunts our spiritual growth—keeping our blinders on and earplugs in.
- We pollute our sentences.
- We move out of our joy alignment.
- We compromise our integrity.
- People cannot trust us to be someone who honors our word.
- We are not doing our part by staying in the truth and the light.
- We are stealing someone's right to hear the truth.

Illuminating the Bad Is Also Good

Illuminators can also light up our path by showing us something our egos don't want to us to know, address, or experience. They can place a situation in front of us that we may perceive as good or bad. Even if it seems bad, it is still good. Whether we personally experience a tragedy or have heard of someone who has, and if the situation drives us to create an organization, start a movement, or change direction in a positive way that touches our life or the lives of others, then the lesson from the tragedy has been learned. We have turned it into a blessing and opened the opportunity to bring in goodness rather than staying stuck in the tragedy itself.

When we allow the depths of our pain to move and lift us in positive ways, we become like the mythical Phoenix that rises from the earth with peace, joy, love, and truth to create miracles in the lives of others with our contagious light and our passion for our purpose. Our loving actions may bring illumination and inspiration to souls in our society that desperately need our specific loving contribution or the organization we created solely as a result of a traumatic and/or painful event we experienced and lived through. The heart-shaped roots we plant deep in the ground during our mission's humble, love-based inception allow our love to flow up and out freely; this love brings souls together and creates a magnified movement of many bringing peace and purpose on the heels of our tragedy.

Ferris Wheel versus Rollercoaster

What happens when we begin living in the truth?

Truth allows us to see everything from all angles. Think of a Ferris wheel as a metaphor for living in the truth vibration location.

When we are seated on a Ferris wheel, we begin at the lowest point and can't see much, but as the wheel—our consciousness—begins to rise, we become increasingly aware of our surroundings as we continue to go higher and higher. Once we reach the pinnacle, pure truth, we gain clear sight, which allows in pure wisdom, and we gain a bird's-eye view as far as our eyes can see. With each turn of the Ferris wheel we gain more perspective and strength. And then we bring that perspective with us as we return to earth.

What happens when you live in a world of deception and lies?

Deception gives us blurry vision or keeps us in the dark altogether. Think of a rollercoaster as a metaphor for living in the untruth vibration location. A rollercoaster starts off slow, but once it gains speed, picking up more energy as it rolls along, it appears as if nothing can stop it. It continues moving quickly, with jerking motions. A rollercoaster allows us only a split second to see and process one or two bits of information before it zooms off in another direction through a dark tunnel at lightning speed.

Similarly, many times deceptive words or actions start off slow, but gain momentum as the negative energy rolls along. The habit of speaking fast actually promotes the telling of untruths, for it allows lies to roll off our tongue quickly and many times unconsciously without our having had a chance to reel them back in or prevent them from going out altogether.

Slowing down our speech and actions places us in the driver's seat, allowing us to remain conscious and in control of our behavior.

Little Lies and Big Lies
Hold the Same Lie Vibration

In the discussion above, I mentioned the truth vibration location and the untruth vibration location. A vibration is an energy resonance. A location is a place. If you understand we are all energy then a vibration location is a place where you have decided to place your energy for that specific moment in time. Truth has a high, light, positive resonance. All lies, regardless if we think they are little or big, hold the same heavy, dark, and negative resonance. Many times little lies form the foundation of another lie, and each lie told builds on its predecessor and gains power and strength along the way. Just as a rollercoaster gains speed as it travels along, so do lies unless they are stopped in their tracks.

Any negative situation you can think of must have a starting point. In most cases it begins with a little white lie, or what's deemed a small deception. For example, a shopaholic doesn't acquire a three-thousand-dollar-per-month spending addiction on his or her first trip to the store. It starts with a secret purchase here and there, followed by small excuses or lies to cover up the behavior, allowing temptations to rule instead of the heart. Such lies build in strength when unchecked behind a wall of deception and go on to create drama and destruction with far-reaching impact.

*"You may use my shield to transmute anything
negative that comes your way and turn it
into something positive."*

— Molly Friedenfeld's channeled message from Archangel Michael

Stealing a Person's Right to Hear the Truth

Did you know when we lie to someone we are stealing? Lying to another is stealing another person's right to hear the truth, and all souls deserve to hear the truth. Lies break down trust in our relationships. We become known as untrustworthy people.

If this doesn't ring true for you, reflect back to a time in your life when someone lied to you and remember how you felt when the deception was revealed. Most likely one or all of three things occurred, which could have been prevented if the truth were presented:

- You were cheated out of something you felt you deserved.
- It created unnecessary drama or hurt your feelings.
- An incident with negative repercussions resulted.

People who tell untruths are easily deceived because they have placed their energy in that negative vibration location and are now a match for that behavior.

SIMPLE HUMAN TRUTH
People who tell untruths are easily deceived because they have placed their energy in that negative vibration location and are now a match for that behavior.

Spiritual Colors

Earlier I referred to Illuminators, the Lightworkers of this world. Light literally creates the color spectrum, and each color has a different vibration.

Positive vibration colors include:

- White—truth
- Yellow—joy
- Blue—kindness
- Green—healing
- Pink and red—love from the heart
- Violet and purple—honor, virtue, spirituality

Negative vibration colors include:

- Black—lies, drama, deceit, spite, anger, and resentment
- Grey—indecision

Avoiding Spiritual Quicksand

If we view lies as black, truth as white, and indecision as grey, it can help us to understand that in order to gain pure sight and pure wisdom, a defining decision must be made. Are we going to live as people of truth, people of deception, or in between worlds in the grey zone?

Perhaps from what you have read so far you are thinking, "I don't lie that much, but I don't always to tell the truth either." If we live life this way, in the grey zone, we stand on a shifting ground called *spiritual quicksand*. When our feet are positioned in spiritual quicksand we are immobile, yet malleable. We may be stubborn, not wanting to see another soul's point of view. And yet, conversely, we may be persuaded to do things we later regret.

We may also allow others to cause us pain by leaving our spiritual doors wide open instead of installing loving boundaries and filters for truth so that we are not giving away our power.

Indecision puts us in the grey zone. It creates the vibration of lack of conviction, compassion, and purpose. When we live with indecision, we attract indecisive people into our world. These are souls who will be honest when it fits their needs and dishonest when it doesn't. Once we define our core integrity, we define what kind of life we want to live, and this process allows others to know our true character and constant intentions at all times. Living with conviction gives us the stable footing we need to build a firm foundation of truth in our lives. With a firm foundation, we are not easily persuaded to veer off the path of truth by the idle temptations of the material world.

Something Smells Fishy, Identifying the Forms of Lying

We use many sayings to "out" deception: "I smell a rat," "I think something is brewing," and "Something smells fishy." Each of these statements implies, "I don't see the deception yet, but I can tell something is going on." It's important to be able to identify the different types of untruths that match the lie vibration; this helps us to hear, see, and feel the negative energy resonance so we can break the pattern of deception.

SIMPLE HUMAN TRUTH
Lies are like anchovies in a Caesar salad. You may not be able to see them, but your soul knows they are there.

Forms of lying include:

- Lying to others—making false statements, giving false information, engaging in false behavior
- Lying to ourselves—not seeing, hearing, or feeling the truth regarding our health, relationships, patterns, or addictions
- Pre-meditated lying—planning deception that will occur in the future
- Exclusion lying—leaving out vital information
- Spontaneous lying—lying when it suits our needs on a moment's notice

LYING TO OTHERS

My decision to break my own pattern of lying and begin living in the truth began about five years ago. I was on my way to show another round of potential homes to a real estate client. I was running late, as usual. I jumped in my car and got my client on the phone, producing a lie during the first thirty seconds of the conversation to cover up the reason for my upcoming tardiness. I quickly stated that I was running fifteen minutes late and had been tied up on the phone with another client. The lie rolled off my tongue with ease, as I had been using this particular *little white lie* for years and had become quite adept at the delivery.

The truth of the matter was, I wasn't tied up on the phone. I was, in fact, putting in one last load of laundry, knocking another thing off my daily "to do" list, and had completely lost track of time. The moment I ended the call, something didn't feel right in my stomach. I thought to myself, "Why would I lie over something silly like that or, to be honest, *anything*, for that matter? Wouldn't honesty be easier?" I began to understand: A lie is a lie, big or small. It's still a violation of truth.

LYING TO OURSELVES

When we lie to ourselves, our ego is in charge. We are living with spiritual blinders on. We arrive at a place of comfort in the shadows by making conscious decisions not to hear, see, or feel the truth. The moment someone arrives on the scene with truth to further our soul's growth, we put up a shield to deflect the information so we don't have to make any changes. Each time the truth is delivered, we push it away.

The good news is, the moment we decide to see, hear, or feel true wisdom and begin living from our hearts, our Angels put a hammer in our hand to assist us in breaking through the barrier we may have created so that we can begin to experience all things spiritual and wonderful.

PREMEDITATED LYING

Any form of planning or orchestrating deception that will violate another soul intentionally at a future time is a form of premeditated lying. Fortunately, our souls constantly give us clues in the form of "pauses in motion" and our Angels and Guides provide synchronistic learning opportunities to teach us how this type of lying adversely affects everyone involved.

Here is one example of the pause in motion: When I was seventeen years old, I called my mother to ask if I could sleep over at my friend Jessica's house. The truth is, I was planning on staying out all night at a boy's house party. I had planned the untruth I was going to tell her, but I noticed a momentary pause before the words came out of my mouth. I had one last chance to tell the truth, but I didn't. I made the *choice* to lie.

EXCLUSION LYING

Exclusion lying involves excluding facts or other vital information from a conversation in which all parties involved need truthful information in order to be able to make the correct decisions.

Here is another personal example: As you may recall, at one point I simultaneously started on a new career path, experienced the passing of my father, and ended my first marriage. My daughter Mallory, granddaughter Hailey, and I were more than ready for things to normalize in our lives. So we were happy when we found a great little townhome on the west side of town, fifteen minutes closer to Minneapolis. We signed a year lease and moved in.

I was out of town when the frantic call came in from my daughter just a few months after we had settled into the townhome. There was a man at our front door, a representative from the bank. The landlord had been taking our rent money but not paying his house payment. The townhome was being foreclosed. We would be uprooted and have to move again.

This story shows why excluding information holds the same vibration as a lie. If the landlord had presented the fact that he wasn't making his house payments at the time we signed the lease, we would have found a different place to rent and never have moved into his rental property in the first place.

You can identify exclusion lying when you find yourself saying:
- "Why didn't you tell me all this before?"
- "If I knew all the information that has now been revealed, my decision would have been different."

IGNORING OR EXCLUDING DETAILS IN CONVERSATIONS

We have probably all experienced the frustration of sending an e-mail or leaving a voicemail asking someone specific questions, only to receive a return message with, say, two of five questions answered. As I learned firsthand, this pattern of avoidance is one of the easiest patterns to fall into.

To encourage someone to acknowledge important questions rather than avoiding them or excluding information, try these tips:

- Highlight, number, or assign bullet points to your questions so they do not get lost in the rest of your message.
- If you have numbered your questions and the recipient has avoided addressing them, hold this person accountable by replying to the e-mail or phone call, highlighting the questions that went unaddressed, and politely mentioning the discrepancy: "Two of the five questions were answered. Could you please respond to the other three?"

There are other types of ignoring or excluding details in conversations, which include:

- Sending a text message from another person's phone without letting the recipient know who you are
- Ignoring a phone message or e-mail altogether

If you get a phone call, voicemail, e-mail, or text from someone with whom you do not want to speak, ignoring the communication actively creates drama. To stay current and in a positive vibration, a simple reply might be, "I saw that you called, e-mailed, or texted. We can talk later. I'm just not ready to discuss this right now."

SPONTANEOUS LYING

Have you ever been approached by a friend who invites you to one of their upcoming jewelry, cosmetic, or gold-exchange parties and, instead of answering truthfully that you'd rather not attend, you lie and say you'll be there, or even fail to respond because you don't want to hurt this person's feelings?

By telling a simple untruth like this, we create complex drama. Why? Because the person now thinks you can make it and is planning on your attendance in her number count for the party. If five people responded with the same untruthful answer, the host's number count could be way off, resulting in an excessive amount of food and disappointing attendance.

Declining invitations with an honest answer demonstrates kindness and truth. A kind response might be, "I have been invited to many parties like this over the years, and I'm going to sit this one out. I appreciate your asking, but that opportunity isn't right for me."

Telling the simple truth has many positive results:

- The person knows your truthful answer.
- She attains a correct number count for attendees and prepares an appropriate amount of food.
- She has an opportunity to ask another person to the party.
- Drama is avoided.

Making Excuses for Not Telling the Truth

Even knowing the importance of telling the truth, we still may avoid doing so. For example, for many years I held a pattern of excluding information from my mother because I felt she worried too much. I believed she was too fragile to handle the truth, and I didn't want her to worry about me unnecessarily. What I didn't realize was that by trying to "protect" her from the truth, I was actually perpetuating and intensifying her worry and fear. Without dispensing the truth, I was creating drama. The pattern of excluding information I had initiated prompted her to begin her own pattern of filling in the blanks with scenarios of things that had never occurred, or flashing forward and worrying about things that had not even had a chance to take place.

Here's an example of how I began to break this pattern:

Two years ago, I visited my mother at her apartment in New Hope, Minnesota on a swelteringly hot and humid day. I announced at the end of my visit that I was heading south of the Twin Cities to visit with a girlfriend I hadn't seen in a long time. My mother immediately asked, with concern in her voice, "Are you sure you want to go anywhere on a day as hot as this? Do you think that is safe?"

By this point, I had reached the understanding that staying in alignment with truth will always illuminate the path of another soul's journey. To help assuage her fears, I kindly replied with the truth using simple, succinct facts: "I have a new car with air conditioning. I also have a cell phone should I run into any problems. Technology is all around us. I will be safe and comfortable on my journey."

Just as I did with my mother, we make many excuses for not telling someone the truth:

- She's too young.
- She's too old.
- He's too rich.
- He's too poor.
- He doesn't want to hear the truth.
- She can't handle the truth.

- He's too ill and fragile.
- She's mentally unstable.
- She will worry too much.
- He already has enough problems.
- She's too preoccupied.

The reality is that every soul deserves the truth—no matter what the circumstances—and will be better for it.

SIMPLE HUMAN TRUTH

Staying in alignment with truth will always illuminate the path of another soul's journey.

***

Once we identify the different ways of telling untruths, we can see how dishonest patterns have become unconsciously woven throughout our daily lives, creating webs of deception that catch all participants in sticky drama. The more the truth is illuminated, the greater our soul's desire to break untruthful patterns and resist societal "shoulds." This desire and intent continue to move us in a positive direction: deeper into our hearts. Thus we begin the process of creating a daily walk of truth, transforming *our* souls and *all* souls.

TRANSFORMING SOULS

This is perhaps the simplest image in the book, a gentle sunrise peeking out across the water, stretching its new rays out over the Earth. It is the dawn of the Age of Truth. It holds all Love, all Joy, and all Wisdom. Its vibration feels a lot like what one feels when they sigh, "Ahhhhhhhhhhh." The Dawn of Truth signifies the end of tolerating what does not work or is not good for humanity or the earth, and instead living from the heart and holding each other responsible for living from the heart in everything we do moving forward.

Transforming Souls

You need not be thrashed about in a boat on a stormy sea. You can connect with the Creator of all that is at any time, which allows you to be present in the moment. In that calm place, you will find the inner wisdom that allows you just to BE.

Showing Houses without Humans

When the home-foreclosure rates skyrocketed in 2007, so did the number of vacant homes that were placed back on the market as "bank owned" inventory. At the time, the banking industry had not yet installed systems to track or manage this new flood of homes. Quite frustratingly to real estate agents like me, there were also no systems in place to let us know whether or not a house was occupied. I began to encounter vacant home after vacant home. I called this new phenomenon *showing houses without humans*. It hurt my heart to think of the sad stories behind each of these empty houses. Also, these vacant homes often had no electricity. No electricity meant no lights.

Whenever I had to show a house without electricity at night, I would use a flashlight to illuminate the different rooms for my clients. Or, if they preferred, I would schedule another showing for when it was light outside. You can't effectively tour a home in the dark. No clients ever wrote up a purchase agreement with me unless they had been able to view a property when it was completely illuminated, because they wanted to discern all the facts about it before making an offer.

The same principle applies when we are delivering information to others. We need to be people of truth and illuminate the facts so another can see all information clearly and make appropriate decisions.

Cancel Out Darkness with Light

Here is another metaphor to help explain the importance of illuminating the truth. Have you ever flipped the switch at the top of the basement stairs and discovered that the light bulb is out? What is the immediate human reaction? We pause at the top of the stairs, in a state of apprehension because there is no light to illuminate the way. After all, dark basements can be scary; the unknown lurks below. Conversely, if you flip the switch and the light bulb goes on, you then proceed down into the illuminated basement without a second thought. There is no pause in motion because you know what lies ahead.

The same thing happens when we face a lie with the truth. Lies are dark. Truth is light. Truth illuminates our path; there is no need to pause when we are afforded the facts. It is always our choice whether we choose darkness over light.

SIMPLE HUMAN TRUTH
When it's dark, turn on the light!
Positive actions always illuminate the darkness.

Transformers

Transformers are souls who illuminate the path for another by facing any negative situation with a positive response.

Transformers are powerful creators of positivity, they can:

- Cancel deceit with truth
- Cancel cheating with honesty
- Cancel doubt with faith
- Cancel apathy with compassion
- Cancel betrayal with loyalty and integrity
- Cancel despair with hope
- Cancel ignorance with knowledge
- Cancel drama with peace and kindness
- Cancel hatred with love
- Cancel discord with harmony
- Cancel injury with justice, fairness, and forgiveness
- Cancel sorrow with joy and gratitude

Our Words Are Alive

If we become conscious that our words are "alive," it can help us to understand this truth that when we tell a lie and speak unkindly toward another, we breathe life into our negative words, creating a strong negative vibration. This creates a breeding ground for continued negative behavior and drama. Simply by switching our thoughts to the positive, we thus begin to switch our words and our vibration to the positive as well. Conscious positive wording assists us in maintaining our joy and a positive outlook on life. It allows us to make the choice to be consciously joyful and consciously grateful for all life experiences.

SIMPLE HUMAN TRUTH

Conscious positive wording assists us in maintaining our joy and a positive outlook on life. It allows us to make the choice to be consciously joyful and consciously grateful for all life experiences.

The Mobile Smokestack

When we work on canceling out darkness (lies and negativity) with light (truth) we become responsible for our energy and take an active role in cleaning up lie pollution. Once, I had a literal experience that made this point clear. On a beautiful clear day in May 2012, I drove across town to visit Mallory and Hailey. I was traveling at 60 mph, soaking in the sun-drenched afternoon and admiring the brilliant blue sky out my front windshield. As I readied myself to change lanes, I looked in the rearview mirror and noticed a red car approaching very quickly behind me. I also noticed immediately—it was unavoidable, really—that the car was spreading an enormous plume of grey smoke out its tailpipe.

As the car passed on my left, the smoke billowing out of the tailpipe engulfed every lane of the highway and obscured my vision of the blue sky. All I could see was dingy grey smoke. I trailed behind this mobile smokestack in its cloud of dingy smoke until exiting the highway one mile up the road. Once I made my turn, I was greeted once again by the brilliant blue sky. I said, "Thank you" to the Universe for returning to me the beautiful gift of clear sight.

Like that mobile smokestack, lies pollute. They pollute our sentences and create a smokescreen that obscures true vision.

Lies and drama are inextricably linked—you don't experience one without the other. The telling of untruths can take a once-pure conversation or sentence and pollute it, nullifying the entire experience.

The great news is that love and truth reign. Face anything untrue with truth, and you drive right through the pollution and receive the gift of clear sight once again.

Become Your Own Programmer

Unfortunately, this metaphorical pollution is all around us. TV reality-show producers seem to have decided that real-life drama and pain inflicted upon others in the guise of good clean fun is entertaining. Viewers are not helping; it seems the more salacious the drama, the higher the ratings. Most of these reality shows seem to be based on deception and backstabbing. There is even a show focused on infidelity, in which souls are caught in the act of cheating on their significant others.

These negative themes appear not only on television, but in all forms of media. We are constantly bombarded by acts of cruelty and deception. People sing about it, write about it, post about it, and talk about by every means available.

To put oneself on the bullet train for spiritual growth, we must become our own programmers. That means making the choice to turn off the media that vibrate with this kind of deceitful and unloving behavior. Creating a new world movement of peace, joy, love, and truth means we must choose the light over the darkness. We have to fan the flame of our inner light that, once re-ignited, creates a burning desire to reject the negative and say, "This has no place in my home or my world."

To make a new world of difference, a soul has to be willing to say, "Starting today, I'm going to be the one to make changes in a positive direction regardless of what other souls around me may be doing." Once we know that *we* are the creators, we can go on to become the Peacemakers in our world. It is our choice.

Setting the Truth Intention

Intention is vital if we are to bring about change and flow all that is good and positive into our lives. When we make the decision to live a truthful life, we are also making the conscious decision to raise our overall awareness and vibration location to that of joy. Truth brings in a simplified way of life. Simple living helps to eliminate drama. Drama-free living = JOY.

We can begin to break the habit of telling untruths by following these simple tips:

ASK FOR DIVINE GUIDANCE

Ask God and your Angels and Guides each morning to help slow down your speech as you work on breaking the pattern of telling untruths. We have a habit of moving fast and talking fast. When we slow down our speech, we have more time, which prevents us from letting lies roll off our tongue without conscious thought. This process sets our soul's intention to tell the truth.

PLACE YOUR HAND OVER YOUR HEART WHEN SPEAKING

While you work on breaking the pattern of telling untruths, place your hand over your heart when speaking. This helps to ground your message in love and truth.

SPEAK INTENTIONALLY

Become word conscious. Make each word count. Strive to break the habit of talking just to fill in the silence. Strive to keep thoughts, words, and actions in truthful alignment. This practice forms our core integrity.

STRUCTURE SENTENCES SO THEY ARE TRUTHFUL

Structure all your sentences so there is no untruth contained within your communication to another.

Let's say I received an invitation to a friend's dinner party and decided not to go. I didn't want to hurt my friend's feelings, so I gave in to the temptation to tell an untruth to cover up the reason for my absence. But I had another choice.

Untruthful sentence: "I'm sorry I didn't go to your party the other night. Peter, my husband, was not feeling well."

Truthful sentence: "I'm sorry I didn't go to your party the other night. We didn't feel like going out that night. We decided to stay home."

BE AWARE OF CLICKS, HICCUPS AND PAUSES

When we are about to lie or perform a deceitful act, our soul will always give us a millisecond to reconsider in the form of a click or hiccup—a momentary pause in action. This pause is an opportunity for our spirit to realize it is always our personal decision whether or not to tell an untruth or perform a deceitful act toward another soul.

LOOK PEOPLE IN THE EYE WHEN SPEAKING

It is difficult to lie when looking another soul in the eyes. As the saying goes, the eyes are the windows of the soul. Truth resides there.

AVOID EMBELLISHING STORIES

Stick with the facts in order to deliver pure truth. (This was a big one for me to overcome. I loved to fill in details that didn't exist to make my stories juicier.) Embellishment may seem harmless, but it holds the lie vibration.

SPEAK NO ILL

As mentioned earlier, when we speak mean-spiritedly about someone, we are, in fact, being mean spirits. All souls are of light and love, so speaking ill of someone is the essence of lying.

Imagine that each conversation you have about another soul, in or out of that person's presence, will be recorded and made accessible for him or her to hear after the fact. Doing this exercise before speaking prevents us from being mean spirits by telling stories about another using information that is not factual or is unkind.

CORRECT YOUR BODY LANGUAGE

Whenever we roll our eyes or shake our heads during a conversation, we sit in judgment of the actions or words of another. Can you ever think of a time when you were in agreement with someone and made those gestures? Most likely, the answer is no. These two forms of body language occur only when we are non-verbally telling someone, "You are wrong and I know what is right."

When you find yourself rolling your eyes or shaking your head over something someone has said or done, place your hand over your heart and say, "Cancel, replace with LOVE." This statement cancels out the judgmental behavior and immediately replaces it with love. Learning to live from our heart space keeps our hearts open wide, which allows us to respect all souls' paths and all stages of learning on each individual journey.

NEVER ASSUME

Breaking the pattern of telling untruths moves us one step closer to eliminating unnecessary drama from our lives. Another way to eliminate drama can be accomplished quite simply by becoming a truth detective.

I'm a fact gatherer and a detective by nature, and most of my occupations have required me to pay great attention to the smallest of details. This has taught me that seeing my way to the truth eliminates drama. That is why it's important never to assume. Assuming is a form of giving away your power to another regarding an outcome that concerns you. Be your own best advocate and seek your own truth by getting all the facts on the table first before making a decision.

Identifying clues that you've assumed include statements like:
- "I thought they were going to take care of it."
- "I just assumed Bob had all the answers, since he handled it last time."
- "I really didn't take the time to ask how they were going to come up with the money."

Here are some tips on how to become a truth detective:
- Ask pertinent questions.
- Go right to the source and talk to all souls involved in the situation at hand.

- Allow only factual, black-and-white information to be gathered, delivered, or taken into account during the decision-making process. Leave no grey areas.

SIMPLE HUMAN TRUTH

Assuming is a form of giving away your power to another regarding an outcome that concerns you.

Staying Conscious Prevents Stretching the Truth

Now that you have set the intention to eliminate drama and the telling of untruths, it is important to stay conscious in order to break this pattern completely. To do this, try the rubber-band method. Place a large, loose rubber band around your wrist and give it a good snap anytime you tell an untruth or speak unkindly about another soul. Wear this rubber band for three to four weeks. Remember, each time you tell an untruth of *any* kind, or speak unkind words about another, give it a good snap. This *snaps* you into consciously acknowledging the untruth. If a welt forms within a few days, it will be a physical reminder of the negative impact any untruth has on your life and on your precious relationships.

(*Note:* If someone should ask you why you are wearing a rubber band, be your authentic self and explain. Telling the truth will give you the opportunity to let everyone know about your exciting truth project.)

SIMPLE HUMAN TRUTH
If you want to know if someone is lying to you,
start by living a truthful life. Once you live in the truth,
you will not be easily deceived.

Start a Truth Journal

Writing in a truth journal is another excellent tool you can use to document experiences, situations, and lessons learned on your journey. Consider using a truth journal in conjunction with your rubber-band project. Each time you snap your rubber band, which means you have told an untruth, stretched the truth, fabricated a story, or said something mean-spirited, write a short description of the incident in your journal. Note the date, time, and details of the untruthful act. Feel free to jot down any feelings that may flow in as you are writing.

Keeping this journal is not about punishing yourself or creating a negative time stamp in any way. Its sole purpose is to get in the habit of consciously bringing your soul forward to help you acknowledge the pattern of telling untruths so you can break it.

When you begin the soul project of living in the truth, you will notice yourself filling pages and pages of your journal very quickly. For the first two to three weeks you will most likely need to carry it with you in order to document each occurrence.

But as you begin to break the vibration that has held you in a pattern of telling untruths, you will notice that the number of entries begins to decrease. This gradual change will reinforce the fact that you are making progress. The rate at which you increase your learning and growth will be marked by the rate at which your entries decrease. The extent of your personal progress with your truth journal will be apparent when you go days, then weeks, then months with no entries recorded on your journal pages.

You may find it useful to keep a few notebooks—in your car, in your desk at work, and on the nightstand in your bedroom—and then transfer your notes into one volume. As you travel along your path of truth, you can then look back across the pages and see the immense wisdom you have gained from each experience.

The Power of Reflection

As you continue to move into a life of truth, reflection is an effective teaching tool. God puts reflection in place not to punish us or have us relive wrongs over and over again in our mind, but to allow us to look back in time so we can connect the dots between specific memories to reveal the purpose and meaning behind synchronistic events. Reflection is a good thing. It is through reflection that we can view both the things we did right and the things we did wrong. In a place of reflection, we can process information, which allows us to learn and grow spiritually.

SIMPLE HUMAN TRUTH
Reflection is a good thing. It allows us to look back in time so we can connect the dots between specific memories to reveal the purpose and meaning behind synchronistic events.

Emancipation Truth Proclamation

The truth is liberating. Revealing your new freedom and personal walk of truth by telling others about it speeds up the process of breaking old patterns. By not keeping others in the dark about your goals, you are being your new, authentic self. Telling others also allows these souls to help you in breaking negative untruth patterns, holding you accountable with love when you fall down. Plus, it gives them insight into a new concept that might propel them to live a life of truth alongside you! Simply tell everyone in your life, "I am making a commitment to live a life of love and truth. Let me know whenever you see me living counter to this intention." This is your *Emancipation Truth Proclamation*.

Divine Friends Show Up to Hold You Accountable for the Truth

Once you put out to the Universe your Emancipation Truth Proclamation, be aware of the Divine Friends that will be placed in front of you frequently by God and your Angels and Guides. Divine Friends are fellow humans who are invested in your learning. They are there to help you identify untruths and break patterns or habits that do not serve your soul as you grow and learn on this wonderful new path.

Please be advised, however, that they may be some of your toughest spiritual teachers. They will test you regarding all the different untruth scenarios you may fall prey to. People will lie to you. You will lie to others. Don't be hard on yourself or the Divine Friends who are assisting you. Remember, this process is all about learning, growth, forgiveness, and loving others unconditionally while on the path to becoming a new, truthful you. Don't take anything personally.

Also, as you begin to work on breaking the untruth vibration, things may appear more difficult than if you just continued telling untruths. This response is only the illusion of fear causing you to think, "If I make all these changes, then I have to become a different person." This is true. Growth is achieved when the truth is revealed. You *will* become a different person—for the better, and that's great!

The more you practice, the better you will become at recognizing and breaking the current hold this specific illusion of fear may hold in your life. Each lesson that is placed before you and absorbed cements another metaphorical brick in place and becomes part of a strong foundation on which to build your core strength, core integrity, and core values. Embrace your lessons. Living in peace, joy, love, and truth is all that is ever asked of you.

SIMPLE HUMAN TRUTH
Growth is achieved when truth is revealed.

***

As you become a healthier self, your heart space continues to expand. This expansion brings forth your true Lightworker energy. A Lightworker has earned the sacred opportunity to be someone who is present for all souls by holding them accountable with love for the truth. The next chapter will show you how to become a demonstrator of Divine Love by consciously and consistently modeling Divine Truth out in the world.

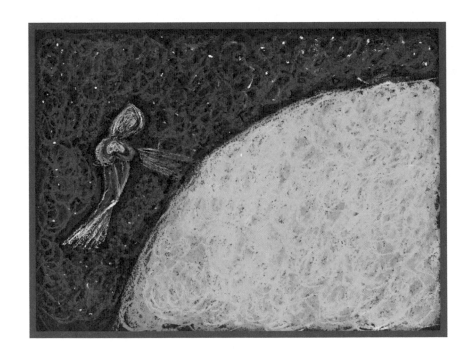

DISCOVERING A NEW WAY TO LOVE

In this image, a soul is looking out across the Universe at the planet Earth. Its hands are folded over the heart and its countenance is filled with love and the knowledge that wisdom, combined with purity of heart, inspires a desire within us to live a life of truth and to illuminate the blessings and benefits of such a lifestyle to others. The soul radiates this knowledge and love to Earth and its inhabitants, willing them to feel the warmth of this heart choice and to embrace it as their new standard of being.

Discovering a New Way to Love

*We have soul contracts with every person in our lives
to live in the vibration of truth.*

Gratitude Brings Peace

Presenting wisdom to another during a difficult time with unconditional love and without judgment is a form of Divine Love. This can
help another soul find meaning and peace behind a tragic event.

One day in May 2010, I received a call from my friend Paula
asking if I would meet her for a spontaneous lunch. I could tell
from the urgency in her voice that she had something important to
tell me. I rearranged my schedule and was soon sitting in a booth
across from her at a restaurant on the other side of town.

Paula began the conversation immediately after we sat down
by recounting a traumatic event that had occurred one month
earlier. She had been at her sister's house with her three-year-old
son, Joshua. He had been playing in the backyard with the family
dog while she watched out the kitchen window. She told me that
her sister had a pool with a tall fence enclosing the entire area. The
moment she mentioned the pool I felt a sense of dread in the pit
of my stomach.

My friend went on to say she had taken her eyes off her son for a few minutes to make sandwiches for lunch when the dog strolled in through the back door. The entrance of the dog triggered Paula to pop her head up from making lunch and look out the back window. A moment of panic struck her when she scanned the area and did not see Joshua in the yard. Adrenaline kicked in, and she sprang into action.

As she flew out the door, Paula realized in horror that the gate of the fence leading to the pool was unlatched.

She told me, "Molly, God was all over the place that day. If my sister's dog had not come in the door at that exact moment, I don't know what would have happened. The pool water was so murky and dark, you couldn't see anything below the surface because they hadn't cleaned the water yet after allowing it to sit all winter."

She continued with a quavering voice, "When I ran out there, I saw Joshua's face just as he was going under the water and was able to pinpoint his location and grab him."

She finished by saying, "At the hospital, I prayed and prayed from the depths of my heart while they warmed him up that he would be all right. My prayers were answered and I have God to thank that my son is all right."

She paused and then continued again, "Molly, the thing is, I cannot get that tragic event and that horrible image out of my head. It keeps playing over and over and over in my mind. I keep seeing the image of my son as he is going under the water. It is with me every minute of the day. I feel like such a horrible mother."

After she had finished, I began to speak slowly, truthfully, and compassionately. I said, "I believe that what you are experiencing is similar to what soldiers go through after they come back from war. It's called post-traumatic stress disorder. That was an incredibly traumatic and stressful event for both you and your son."

My voice cracked as I continued, "I want you to understand that by looping the trauma of that event over and over in your mind you are allowing your mind to rule you instead of your heart. By staying in your head this means you are sending your spirit back in time to relive the pain of that *one* event, and allowing it to build in power so it becomes more like *hundreds* or *thousands* of painful events."

I advised Paula, "Stay right here in the present, with your heart open wide and full of gratitude for the many blessings you received that day. You were given the opportunity to learn many lessons and thank God your son was allowed to live through those lessons. You can now turn this experience into a positive one and go on to bless others facing similar struggles or teach others about pool safety."

I continued, "You can even help others see how God is always there, guiding us and giving us clues through Divine Synchronicities, like your sister's dog coming through the door at the perfectly orchestrated time, and how you saw your son the second before he went under the water, which allowed you to find him."

I concluded, "Our hearts are where God resides." I then put my hand over my heart and said, "It is now your conscious choice in which direction you choose to travel. Please try to travel to a place of gratitude every time you see your son's face. This way you can remember the gift you received instead of the son you almost lost."

Understanding the lesson from a significant life event allows peace to follow. Once we arrive at the place in our lives where we desire pure truth and wisdom to be brought forth in our learning process, we are willing to see all vantage points and the many synchronicities that occur—both during an event and leading up to it. Understanding the Divine Learning process is what brings us back into alignment with our soul's essence, love. The more adept we become at feeling love and gratitude for all life's earthly learning experiences, the more quickly we are reminded that, whatever hardship may be placed before us, it is *our choice* always to return to a place of love and gratitude and to give thanks for all that still remains.

SIMPLE HUMAN TRUTH

The more adept we become at feeling love and gratitude for all life's earthly learning experiences, the more quickly we are reminded that, whatever hardship may be placed before us, it is our choice always to return to a place of love and gratitude and to give thanks for all that still remains.

Dispensing the Truth in Business

When you are demonstrating Divine Love by dispensing the truth, it may fall on ears that are not ready to hear your message of wisdom at the time. As this next story demonstrates, whether someone likes the information or not, when the truth is dispensed it is for the good of all, always.

In the late 2000s, as housing prices continued to plummet around the country, my job as a real estate agent became increasingly difficult. This was especially so if a client needed to sell a home rather buy one. In the course of doing business, I often had to speak difficult truths.

I remember a listing appointment I had with a Minneapolis couple named Jack and Beverly. After running the home sales reports, I noticed that housing prices were dropping precipitously in their area and told the couple they had a very small window in which to get their house sold before prices dropped further. Jack and Beverly's house was built at the turn of the century and was very expansive. My partner and I kindly pointed out needed repairs and items in need of full disclosure so a potential buyer would be informed of the home's overall condition.

Part one of my truthfulness mantra for listing appointments was to make sure the clients were aware of current pricing by showing them home sales reports, which present the truthful recorded prices of closed homes sales in their area.

Part two of my mantra was always to state simply, "If you were a potential buyer and you were going to purchase this home, what are the things you would like disclosed to you? What are the things that would make you angry if you weren't informed about them?"

Part three was to remind the clients of the Golden Rule. I would finish by stating, "Treat others as you would like to be treated—as if the shoe were on the other foot and you were buying this home—and you will have a very successful and drama-free transaction."

Three weeks later, my partner and I found out that we did not get the listing business on Jack and Beverly's home. Upon hearing this, I thought to myself, "I did my job. I delivered the truth."

It would be four years before I would find out that our truthful delivery had indeed made a difference—through a synchronistic conversation with Angie, a friend I ran into who knew the potential clients.

She told me, "Do you remember that listing appointment you went on for my friends Jack and Beverly from Minneapolis? They didn't like what you had to say at the time you met with them, but when I talked to Beverly recently she mentioned you. She said,

'You know, everything Molly told us was the truth. We should have listened to her.'"

SIMPLE HUMAN TRUTH
When the truth is dispensed it is for the good of all, always.

Thou Shalt Not Take Anything Personally

When you have a strong connection with the Divine, it's important to stay firm in your faith and dedicated to doing what's right regardless of what others around you are doing. As my last story shows, there may be times that others may become upset with you as a result of your truthful decisions or the truthful information you may have lovingly dispensed. Living in the truth can make other people uncomfortable as you shine the light on things with which they may not be ready to, or do not want to, address. At such times, have faith in this simple knowledge: Everything is placed in front of each soul in Divine Order with Divine Timing. There is a synchronistic lesson to be learned in every encounter to further the growth of each soul involved. The Universe does not orchestrate one-sided lessons.

Pure truth is always present, but it is each soul's choice to decide when he or she wants it to be revealed. So if someone does not want to hear the truth, don't take it personally. Just keep doing what you are doing. Remain on the side of peace, joy, love, and truth. Have faith in knowing that by doing God's work and staying in the light, *you* are learning and growing, too! You are also playing a very important role in upholding the truth for the collective consciousness. You are helping humanity. This is far more important than any small amount of discomfort you may experience at the hands of another who is not ready to hear the truth at the time it is dispensed.

SIMPLE HUMAN TRUTH

Pure truth is always present, but it is each soul's choice to decide when he or she wants it to be revealed.

Gatekeepers, Border Guards, and Triangle Creators

Holding all souls accountable for the truth with love means we may also need to help another see their way to the truth by shining the light on negative relationship patterns that are breeding grounds for drama and deception. One of the main reasons negative relationship patterns develop is because one or more persons in a relationship have taken it upon themselves to become a guardian—one who prevents another from hearing, seeing, or being responsible for upholding the truth.

The three different types of guardians are:

- Gatekeeper
- Triangle Creator
- Border Guard

A *Gatekeeper* is a person who feels he or she needs to be in charge of the information disseminated among a group or to a specific person rather than allowing others to find their own way to the truth. A Gatekeeper may also filter information by allowing only partial truth to be dispensed. He or she can effectively prevent people from walking through their own learning experiences, especially if a painful lesson is to be learned, which may prevent all souls involved from experiencing their own life lessons.

Examples of Gatekeeper statements:

- "I didn't tell her about what happened at the meeting. She's too fragile to hear that kind of bad news."
- "You let me tell him. He doesn't need to hear this coming from you."
- "I made the decision for him."

A *Border Guard* is a person who wants to police another person from taking a stand for truth or integrity.

Examples of Border Guard statements:

- "Whatever happens, do not mention that you know Sherry stole money from your purse. That will just make the situation worse."
- "I don't think holding Jerry accountable for showing up ten minutes late to work every day by reporting him to the boss is going to make any difference. Is it really that big of a deal if you just stay a few minutes later each day until he arrives?"
- "You had no right to tell Sam the truth, even if he asked you directly."

A *Triangle Creator* is a person who likes to stir the pot in many different ways, bringing souls into the mix who are directly, indirectly, or not at all involved in a situation in order to create drama. The intent is to keep all souls locked under the Triangle Creator's control by controlling how the truth gets revealed.

Examples of Triangle Creator statements:

- "You tell John for me everything I said to you just now."

- "I had Sally listen to your voicemail and she thinks you are wrong, too."
- "I don't know anything about the situation, but if it makes it easier you can make me the bad guy so she isn't mad at you."

Getting the Point Across on Triangles

All triangles create drama, which de-values and sometimes shatters our precious relationships. As this next story shows, many sad stories are created when these triangles are allowed to take shape and grow.

Years ago, a friend told me about a woman named Emily who lived in a neighborhood where husbands and wives (including her) cheated on each other. When I heard this story for the first time I felt a jolt of pain run through my heart. I felt the sadness behind the wall of drama created by these souls, living within an orchestrated triangle of deception among their neighbors. I felt sadness for all the souls involved, especially for the innocent children of these cheating spouses.

Children are empathic little sponges. They sense our emotions and easily pick up on body language, drama, deceit, and negativity in their environment. If you have ever had a child ask you if anything is wrong when you are trying to make everything appear normal, you will recognize the truth of this statement. When a child witnesses or feels inappropriate behavior from parents, it shatters that child's security and damages bonds of loyalty and trust.

One particular aspect of Emily's story demonstrates how very empathetic and perceptive children are. My friend told me of an instance when Emily's young son reprimanded her from his car seat, stating, "Mommy, please stop talking on the phone to that man who isn't my daddy."

Truthful Equations Equal Powerful Solutions

We don't need to be mathematicians to realize it is important for us to speak directly to all souls that are part of the equation in any Gatekeeper, Triangle Creator or Border Guard scenario so that they may choose to become an integral part of the solution. While the variations on each of these drama formulations are endless, the solution to all such negative scenarios is simple. Face each situation with love and truth to end the drama.

If you encounter behavior like this, assist another soul in realizing the damage done to their precious relationships by asking the person's soul to step forward using soul-searching questions. Deliver your question and message with compassion and love and without judgment.

Here are some sample questions to help you get the conversation started:

- "Do you feel this behavior is based in love?"
- "Do you feel this behavior is demonstrating healthy boundaries and relationships for your family life, personal life, or work environment?"
- "Do you think there will ever be a positive outcome for any souls involved if this behavior is allowed to continue?"
- "Do you want this same behavior mirrored back at you?"

Placing Conditions on Love

Another source of negative relationship patterns is conditional love. The only kind of pure love is unconditional love. Conditional love is fear-based. Fear says, "In order to get this, you must do that or else you will be without."

Examples of conditional love:

- "If you tell your mother about this, you can forget about that new bike I was going to buy for you."
- "I will help cover up this mistake for you this one time, but then I expect you to help me in return."
- "I'm not going to say I'm sorry unless he apologizes first."
- "I'm not willing to change unless others start making changes around me."

Staying within your core power, core strength, and core integrity prevents you from giving away your power to an untruth—fear. Facing conditional love with truth helps you to see that any time a stipulation on love is present, unconditional love is not.

SIMPLE HUMAN TRUTH
Any time a stipulation on love is present,
unconditional love is not.

Holding Souls Accountable with Love

Just as with other negative behaviors, when an untruth is told in our presence we can hold a soul accountable by not allowing the opportunity to pass by without a kind and loving correction. This isn't about telling someone he or she is a liar. This is about helping another soul build a desire to live in the truth by breaking old patterns through the pathway of love.

To assist a person in allowing the soul to step forward during a conversation, we must slow that person down in order to bring him or her to a more conscious state. Allow the person to finish speaking. It is important not to interrupt. Then create a pregnant pause and ask one of the following questions:

- "Do you really believe that statement you just made to be true?"
- "Does that statement ring true for you?"
- "Can you repeat that statement so I can make sure I heard your truth correctly?"

Once we choose to walk in the truth, transformational growth begins and wonderful things start to unfold in our lives and in the lives of those around us. Even if the person who speaks an untruth doesn't admit it at the time, or even refuses to see the truth, you have done your job. This process has created a time fragment that will allow the person or their Angels and Spirit Guides the opportunity to flow this event back into their consciousness as a memory at some time in the future. This process is a very effective learning tool, and allows a soul to fit one more piece into his or her life puzzle and to understand the immense value of truthful words.

Holding a soul accountable for the truth tells that person: "I see you; I love you; we are connected; we are helping each other grow."

SIMPLE HUMAN TRUTH
Once we choose to walk in the truth, transformational growth begins and wonderful things start to unfold in our lives and in the lives of those around us.

Patience Is Key When Teaching Others

Dispensing truthful information in small snippets and in a non-judgmental and non-threatening style allows for absorption of wisdom on the soul level. When we are helping someone see the way to the truth in any situation, we can guide that soul with patience, ask questions, and plant seeds of knowledge without preaching. A soul must gain wisdom by gathering information in whatever way works best. It is impossible to force wisdom on another, because each person has a choice to determine how and if it will be received. We Illuminators or Transformers understand that each person may learn at a different speed and we honor all paths.

Things to keep in mind when teaching others:
- Patience is key.
- Guide rather than preach.
- Plant seeds of truth and knowledge with love.

Here are some teaching-the-truth delivery tips:
- Place your hand over your heart when you begin speaking. This movement indicates your intention to become completely present in the conversation and keeps you grounded in the location of love.
- Pepper questions throughout the teaching conversation

instead of using stand-alone statements. This technique creates dialogue and prevents the person in the learning position from feeling as if you are preaching.

"What if…"

"Consider this…"

"Have you ever thought of it this way?"

Example of out-of-alignment teaching:

"When you lie to someone you are doing wrong by people. It's so obvious. Can't you see that?"

Example of in-alignment teaching:

"Consider this for a moment. If you look at the situation and use the Golden Rule, can you understand how you would feel if you found out someone had deceived you by telling a similar untruth?"

SIMPLE HUMAN TRUTH

A soul must gain wisdom by gathering information in whatever way works best. It is impossible to force wisdom on another, because each person has a choice to determine how and if it will be received.

Defensive Deflection to Avoid the Truth

Even if you deliver truth and attempt to teach with love, sometimes a person will resist your message. Remember that anything that is not love is fear-based. *Deflection* is a fear-based tactic many of us use to keep the truth from being revealed or addressed.

Signs of deflection to avoid hearing the truth include:

- Dramatic outbursts and false statements such as: "Stop judging me!"
- Drawing other people into a situation to create drama as a diversion
- Shutting down the conversation by leaving the scene
- Cruel or isolating statements

Examples of isolating statements:

- "You are wrong."
- "I *know* I am right."
- "Your ideas are stupid."

If someone you know uses words like these in their speech, a short, kind, and consistent correction at the time of occurrence can break this pattern over time. Use heartfelt language to get your point across. For example, "When you say to me, 'Your ideas are stupid,' or 'You are right and I am wrong,' that really hurts me. It's isolating language and it shuts down our conversation. I want both of us to learn and change. Let's try to be kind with our words towards one another so we can communicate, with love, more effectively."

SIMPLE HUMAN TRUTH

When someone wants to give you a "piece of their mind,"
ask them to give you "peace from their heart" instead.

Silent Agreement and Silent Participation

When we are involved in a situation and hear untruths spoken or view inappropriate actions and then allow the event to go unchecked without a loving correction, our behavior can be viewed as silent agreement or silent participation. I have attended many wedding ceremonies and have heard the officiant say, "Speak now or forever hold your peace." It is understood that if you don't speak at that moment, you are in silent agreement with the marriage. Similarly, many times we may not agree with something inside, but go along for the ride anyway because we are uncomfortable with speaking our truth. But by becoming a person who takes a stand for love and truth, we begin a love and truth movement.

Here is an example of demonstrating core strength and core integrity instead of simply going along for the ride: A husband named Harry is away on a business trip with important male clients. After dinner, his clients discuss their desire to go to a gentlemen's club as their evening entertainment. Harry is not in agreement. He and his wife have talked about this very subject in depth and he knows it would create a breach of trust and damage to their relationship. Harry speaks his truth without placing judgment on the decisions of the other men by telling them he will not be attending and why.

He states, "Hey, guys, I have to say that for me, going to a club like that does not show love to my wife or my children. We don't keep any secrets in my family, and I know if I told my wife I went to a location like that, it would create damage to our relationship. I'm going to have to split off from the group at this point." This kind truth demonstrates to the other men that Harry is a man with core strength and core integrity who respects his wife and his family unit.

All it takes is one man or woman to stand up for love and truth to break this type of negative pattern. By being present and showing love for his wife in her absence, this one man has demonstrated a love-based relationship of truth to all the men in the group, shown respectful behavior to their wives, and also placed value on the women at the gentlemen's club.

When we view all souls as members of our connected family unit, we become united in love. A possible result is a chain reaction. A statement like Harry's may give another man enough time to gather up his power to say, "Hey, guys, I guess I'm going to sit this one out, too." Thus the movement of love and truth begins. This process also maintains peace and joy, as there will be no lie to cover up the evening's events, thus eliminating drama—and allowing him to stay in a joyful vibration location.

When we lovingly correct untruths or untruthful behavior when it occurs instead of allowing silence to become our nonverbal form of agreement, we accomplish many things:

- We show love to all souls, even those not present.
- We stand firm in our core strength and core integrity by shining the light on a behavior that does not show love or represent the truth.
- We promote soul growth for all parties involved.

SIMPLE HUMAN TRUTH
When we view all souls as members of our connected family unit, we become united in love.

To Tell the Truth, the Whole Truth, and Nothing but the Truth

On your journey to the truth, you may encounter people that will try to trick you into lying by asking difficult questions. Core strength and core integrity allow you to stay truthful even during uncomfortable encounters. If someone attempts to veer you off track, you can easily stay in alignment by answering the question in a way that is truthful for you. A simple truth delivered in kindness may be the impetus that ignites a passionate fire in another's soul and goes on to become the source of motivation for positive change.

Here are some examples:

Question: "Do you think I look fat?"

Answer: "I don't like the word *fat*. It seems to me that you are not at your optimum body weight, and just like me I'm sure you would benefit from an exercise program."

Question: "Do you like my haircut?"

Answer: "The haircut you have is not my style, so your haircut is not right for me. I personally think if we love our hairstyle, we just know it and we feel good about it. I've noticed if I get a haircut and there is anything that feels out of alignment regarding the cut or style, I look to others for approval."

SIMPLE HUMAN TRUTH

A simple truth delivered in kindness may be the impetus that ignites a passionate fire in another's soul and goes on to become the source of motivation for positive change.

Spiritual Housecleaning, Taking a Break from Those We Love

It may be difficult, but there will be times when we need to pick up our brooms and do some spiritual housecleaning. It is through this process that we find our true relationships, our true heart, our core integrity, and our life's purpose. We can find peace along this journey by embracing the change, loving others as we go, and inviting in our new life as it is revealed and flowed to us.

For example, let's say we used to be a person who told many untruths and were friends with people who also told untruths and perhaps even lied to, cheated, or harmed others. Once we realize we want to change and become more loving, evolved souls who live truthful lives, we no longer remain a vibrational match for those souls that wish to stay right where they are. This is the meaning of sayings such as "birds of a feather flock together" and "thick as thieves." "Like-minded" and "like-hearted" souls stick together.

As we work on self-growth and increase our vibration with each piece of new wisdom we absorb, we come to know how wonderful and simple it is to live a truthful and drama-free life. When we receive this revelation, we begin to experience what I call the *disconnection process*. Disconnection occurs when we realize a person or group is no longer a vibrational match for or in alignment with our core integrity. Each encounter with the person or group will begin to feel rough, like sandpaper. We may find ourselves saying, "I just don't enjoy myself when I'm around Sarah. It's not fun anymore. It's actually quite tiring and stressful." It is at this time that we may come to understand that it is not possible to become a new person while hanging on to people or things we may have once held dear but that no longer serve us.

While we are learning, growing, changing, and moving forward, our current friends and family members will either need to work on their own self-growth so they can come along with us, or we may need to leave them in their own vibrational space, temporarily or permanently.

Signs of disconnection are easy to recognize. We may not see eye to eye anymore with certain people. We may even have immediate disagreements within a few minutes of reconnecting with them. Each encounter becomes more uncomfortable, and each time you leave their presence you may feel out of your joy alignment. Others that are not at a similar vibration location on their spiritual paths may not understand this process, but it is part of self-discovery and self-growth. It is unavoidable, so embrace it and work with it when you notice its entrance through your door. This doesn't necessarily mean your friends or specific family members will go away forever, but it might. It all depends on whether we decide to keep moving forward in our own learning while they decide to stay right where they are.

Disconnecting may mean we have family members that we still love dearly but now find it comfortable to see them only around the holidays or on special occasions. It may mean we need to take a break with love from friends that we have known all of our lives. The more this process occurs, the more you will learn about the power of energy and energy shifting. And the more you *allow* instead of trying to *control* change, the easier it is for the Universe to flow wonderful new energy, people, abundance, and experiences your way. So hold out your hands, stretch your arms wide, and say, "Thank you for all that I've experienced so far, and thank you for all that is to come! I am a grateful soul!"

SIMPLE HUMAN TRUTH

*It may be difficult, but there will be times we need to pick
up our brooms and do some spiritual house cleaning. It is
through this process that we find our true relationships, our
true heart, our core integrity, and our life's purpose.*

To begin your spiritual housecleaning, surround yourself
with souls that live with the foundation of core integrity. These
are people that have the desire to live in the truth. They will help
you to raise or maintain your positive vibration location. You
will also find that the more you grow, the more the Universe
flushes out the people that are not a vibrational match for you.
The good news is that the Universe doesn't allow a void. Once
you begin living in the positive truth vibration, the Universe
will show its appreciation by flowing in souls who *are* a vibrational match to enhance your new way of life.

Mind you, I have seen souls go backward at this stage in their
growth. Change will not be easy or comfortable if you are resist-
ing it. Relationships are, many times, the place where one must
truly draw a line in the sand, so to speak. This world is all about
choice. As friends, family members, or the comfortable life you
once knew begin to drop away, you may decide it's too much
change and choose to step backward by lowering your vibration
to the level where you can hold onto those people and things.
I want to caution you, though, that once you have stepped into
the light, the Universe will bombard you with lessons to show
you that stepping backward will create more discomfort than
moving forward toward positive growth.

On a positive note, the other souls with whom you can't bear to part are always welcome to raise their vibration by becoming wiser, kinder, more loving and truthful souls. And when they do, they will come right back into alignment with you and everything will feel good again.

SIMPLE HUMAN TRUTH
Once you begin living in the positive truth vibration, the Universe will show its appreciation by flowing in souls that are a vibrational match to enhance your new way of life.

***

Once we successfully eliminate illusionary living, a fog lifts and we are able to clearly see and discover a wonderful new life infused with these four foundational energetic pillars—Divine Peace, Divine Joy, Divine Love, and Divine Truth. Now that you know this truth, the next chapter will explain the Divine Simplicity and Divine Love of God, and why all roads lead to this same beautiful Source.

ALL ROADS LEAD TO GOD

Imagine the world held lovingly in the hands of God. He holds it, but does not control it. All resources are provided, and all the outcomes and creations from this orb and the souls who inhabit it are celebrated in a tender exchange of loving support and appreciation. The individuals may not know each other, and may not share the same understanding of God and the Universe, but in the language of their hearts there is this commonality: All are connected through their connection to Source; all their roads come from, and return to, this same Source.

All Roads Lead to God

It is through religions, institutions created by humans, that we have made finding God complicated.

All Roads Lead to God

I have friends of many faiths: Jewish, Buddhist, Hindu, Catholic, Methodist, and Lutheran. Regardless of each religion's origin, it seems to me that the ultimate goal of all of these faiths is to find God—to connect with what various people call the Divine, the Holy Spirit, Creator, Higher Power, or Source of All That Is. Just as I can choose to take a different route to work each day, but ultimately pull into the same parking lot at the same office complex at the end of my commute, there are many routes to finding God.

Each person's route is unique. One person's commute may be longer than another's, or more congested by stoplights, turns, and detours, but the end result is the same. We all reach our intended goal, the office. It is the same with spirituality. I can belong to a church, a synagogue, or a temple. I can read the Bible, the Torah, or the Vedas. Each of these ancient texts takes a different route, but by reading them I attain the same goal, finding God.

This is because all roads lead to God. It doesn't matter which path I take to awaken my spirituality on my way back to Source and my soul's essence, love. What is important is that I step onto a path.

SIMPLE HUMAN TRUTH

The spiritual things that you may not be able to see and feel are just as real as the things you can. God puts faith in place so you can believe in Him and all things spiritual without have it set before you in physical form.

Taking Fear and Illusion Out of Religion

I believe some human-made religions may inject fear and complexity into their doctrines to hold their faithful followers back from finding their own truth and their own relationship with God.

Religion can be complex.

Pure truth is simple. Finding God is simple.

It is the ego, and fear of the unknown, that try to convince a soul that one specific religion, culture, or race is the only one of true importance. This type of thinking takes us away from the pure truth that all souls hold value in God's eyes.

Some religions teach with fear at the foundation. Fear is an illusion, an inhibitor, an intimidator, and the ultimate isolator. It has many layers and it opens the door to many different interpretations of reality. These interpretations depend on the person dispensing the fear, his or her own filters or beliefs, and the person willing to receive the illusion of fear. Fear allows distortion of the original intent of religion: to spread pure peace, pure joy, pure love, pure truth, and pure wisdom.

God is pure love. God is pure truth. God is pure wisdom. God is the great networker. He brings together souls with love, not fear. Love goes hand in hand with light, peace, joy, truth, communication, trust, and knowing. There is no fear in love. When we live in the truth, we turn on our own spiritual flashlight and illuminate a direct pathway to God.

SIMPLE HUMAN TRUTH

There is no fear in love. Live with the foundation of LOVE in your heart and you will become FEARLESS.

By God! Heaven Would Be Empty!

I was having a conversation with a friend a while back who told me, "Molly, my religion states we only have one chance in this life to get it right. If we don't, we are going to Hell."

I replied, "I believe earth is one big classroom. We are all here to learn endless lessons. You and I have both told lies, and have hurt and judged people over the years, whether intentionally or unintentionally, right?"

She said, "Yes, of course. We're not perfect."

I went on, "My humble point exactly. We are not perfect; that is why we are here to learn. How do we learn if we don't fall down, make mistakes, and come out the other side a more compassionate, wiser, and loving human?

"If we go with the concept that we are going to Hell if we don't get it exactly right, then by God, Heaven would be empty, as I have not yet encountered a perfect human in my lifetime or anywhere in history."

Within days of that conversation, I had another friend ask, "Tell me how you think God views homosexuals."

I replied, "We are all children of God. I believe each person is God's unique creation. He creates all different types of people to be present before us so we can learn how to become compassionate and non-judgmental souls. What right do we have to judge the chosen path or lifestyle of another? How would we ever learn to be compassionate if we were never afforded the opportunity to show or receive compassion?"

I ended by stating, "I have judged many people incorrectly in my life and have had many people cast judgment on me in return. Looking back, those encounters taught me some of my biggest life lessons."

SIMPLE HUMAN TRUTH
We are not perfect. We are here to learn.
Earth is one big classroom and God is our
heavenly guidance counselor and teacher.

The Golden Rule Simplifies World Religions

I was amazed when I discovered the simplicity of The Golden Rule. Also known as the ethic of reciprocity, this wisdom is found in the scriptures of nearly every religion. The Golden Rule is often regarded as the most concise principle of ethics. Breaking down the similarities between the Golden Rule and the precepts of world religions helps us to see how divinely connected these religions are when we remove fear, denominational barriers, and the filters that keep us disconnected from pure truth.

GOLDEN RULE

"Do unto others as you would have others do unto you."

CHRISTIANITY

"Whatsoever ye would that men do unto you, do you even so unto them."

CONFUCIANISM

"Do not impose on others what you do not wish for yourself."

HINDUISM

"This is the sum of duty; do naught unto others, what you would not have them do unto you."

JUDAISM

"What is hateful to you, do not do to your neighbor: That is the whole Torah; all the rest of it is commentary; go and learn."

ISLAM

"A man should wander about treating all creatures as he himself would be treated."

SIMPLE HUMAN TRUTH
The Golden Rule is often regarded as the most concise principle of ethics.

Afterword

I began the journey of returning to my soul's essence—love—by taking the first step of acknowledging the importance of truth. Truth is my internal guidance system, just like true north on a compass, and acts as a constant form of calibration for my life. This guidance system points the way to clear sight, which in turn allows me to see the importance of breaking through my self-imposed, earthly illusions. What will you decide to do with the truthful wisdom that has been revealed within these pages? Will you go on to become one of the Illuminators and Transformers, instrumental in birthing and spreading the movement of pure truth across the earth with the dawning of each new day? Or will this book become just another that is read and then placed on a shelf and forgotten? The choice is, always, yours. My sincere hope is that these words have created a desire to begin your own spiritual journey and that, with each intentional footstep you take, it will help you to remember why it is you came here and why you don't want to leave without placing your thumbprint of peace, joy, love and truth upon this earth.

Peace and Love,

Molly Friedenfeld

Energetic Exchange

by Cynthia Shepherd

In the spiritual realm there is neither time nor space ... and there is no money. Money is only a shadow of the greater ideal the Universe (God) had in mind when it created this world, intending for us to intermingle and share our unique talents and gifts. So if we are here to bring Heaven to earth, what steps are we willing to take to do that? In pursuit of the original intent, or higher ideal, many spiritual students and seekers are turning to barter, trade, and something known as *Energetic Exchange*.

Energetic Exchange is a form of collaboration that does not necessarily entail money, but still provides a fair and equitable exchange for all parties involved in whatever form those parties feel is appropriate. Other very important aspects of an Energetic Exchange are that it does not stem from ego, and that there are no hidden agendas. In fact, neither of these two things can be present at all, not even a speck, for Energetic Exchange is a product of the heart (the place Heaven resides within us) and wells up naturally from a foundation of love and integrity. It is a blending of loving souls, aligned in their intentions, who give gifts from their hearts as Spirit moves them.

Molly and I love the concept of Energetic Exchange and set out to practice it with each other; this book project evolved organically from that decision and created many opportunities to do just that. We discovered ideas bubbling up one after the other and synchronicities dotting our paths, filling us with awe and delight. Molly and I had already practiced Energetic Exchange on the Violet Wisdom Inspiration Radio show a number of times during the last year; I supplied content for Molly's listeners, helping to build the audience, and her show in turn brought new clients for me. I also spoke at an event Molly hosted, a form of extending the show's content and vibration to the area where she lives, and I gained new clients from that opportunity, too. All the while, the exchanges themselves were full of love, light, and ease. As a bonus, a great friendship was forming between us.

Through the course of these exchanges, and growing closer as friends, Molly and I have realized both how similar our messages are and the vibration that we wish to help generate on this planet. This realization led Molly to decide that my *soul drawings* might be a great addition to her book, helping to anchor the energetic imprint of the concepts she illuminated with her words using images that Spirit channels through me that match their meaning. Molly then asked me to create a set of drawings that represented the soul of each chapter.

The intention we, as two powerful co-creators, wish to share through the combined energy of Molly's heartfelt words and my soul drawings is that no person's value is any more or less important than any other's, and that when we collaborate in integrity and love we can create beautiful magic. We hope you have discovered along your journey through this book that the images really do build off the words, such that you take away the full implications of the concepts we express and are inspired to find ways to help you ground your own life in peace, joy, love and truth. Perhaps you, too, will feel guided to create and collaborate with others using the concept of Energetic Exchange.

We would like to make special mention of Molly's friend David Keyes, who also contributed to this Energetic Exchange by providing his photographic gift for capturing the light and soul of each of my drawings as well as enhancing Molly's personal photos for this book.

About the Author

Molly Friedenfeld is a businesswoman, mentor, spiritual teacher, writer, and successful Internet radio show host. Molly's passion is to motivate and teach others how to live a life with peace, joy, love, truth, and integrity as its foundation. She believes there is no such thing as a coincidence; everything is divinely guided behind the scenes to provide endless spiritual synchronicities throughout our days.

Molly and the love of her life, her husband Peter, live in Minneapolis, Minnesota within a blended family consisting of five other wonderful souls: children Mallory, Maddy, Will, and Jake and granddaughter Hailey.

Violet Wisdom Inspiration Radio:
www.blogtalkradio.com/violet-wisdom

Violet Wisdom website:
www.violetwisdom.com

About the Artist

Cynthia Shepherd is a Certified Master Life Coach, Law of Attraction expert, and a Minister of Peace, as well as a healer, spiritual teacher, artist, and poet. Her channeled "soul artistry" allows the vibrational resonance of Divine Messages to be captured in non-verbal form so the messages essence can be absorbed directly, without having to go through our personal filter system—our mind. She is passionate about finding ways to bring Divine Grace into our lives.

Cynthia Shepherd's website:
www.cynthiashepherd.com

About the Photographer

David Keyes is a commercial and portrait photographer based in St. Paul, Minnesota, specializing in natural light and lifestyle portraiture of children and families. For this book, David supplied his post-processing talents to bring out the most in Cynthia Shepherd's artwork and Molly's personal photos.

David Keyes website:
www.davidkeyesphotography.com